Her Fated Place

JEAN ANDREWS

THE CHOIR PRESS

First published in the United Kingdom in 2023 by
The Choir Press

ISBN 978-1-78963-386-3

Also by Jean Andrews

Poetry
In an Oubliette
Lunatica
Sí-Orphans of the Plaintive Air
The Heron on the Lake
The Muted Blade

Translated Poetry
Nancy Morejón, Black Woman and Other Poems
Carmen Conde, While the Men Are Dying

Website: jeanandrewspoetry.co.uk

Contents

Prologue,
Summer 1937

It is not prudent to watch
Appletrees growing
And in the abundant green orchard
Not to think of nothing.

Brendan Kennelly, 'Uncertainty',
Love of Ireland; Poems from the Irish

The Portrait

Before a folding screen in the orchard,
intricate rosewood and faded carmine plush,
a relic of high collars, cinched waists
and pompadour hair,
Venetia stepped out of her fated place,
a tied cottage on the Atlantic coast,
domestic service on a fading Anglo-Irish demesne.

Waved locks, cropped to the nape of her neck,
sheathed in a satin, sleeveless dress,
head in profile like the backlit star
of George Cukor's *Camille*
with big green eyes dreaming of waltzes,
champagne fountains and beaux,
at seventeen the world was hers to own.

Had she only been born to the titled family
and not the gardener and his nursemaid wife,
she might well have featured in *Debrett's,*
espoused to the scion of a 1066 duke.
Yet her poise belied the inescapable truth:
she must follow in her parents' footsteps,
or *sans* contacts, education or wealth
attempt to forge for herself
a different kind of luck.

I

The Ingenue,
Spring and Summer 1938

The Journey

Ragnallstown, the estate of Sir Finian and Lady (Bella) Fitzmaurice.

When her father took her in the pony and trap
the six miles to catch the Dublin train,
it was as far as she had ever gone from home before
and she left him without a tear or a backward look.
Nine months after the orchard portrait,
with no sign of other work,
like her mother before her
she was to be a nursery maid,
but on the other side of the country,
inland, on the fertile plains.

She was collected from the station
in a similar trap, driven by a lad
who was eighteen, like herself,
not a word of whose slurred Midlands accent
she could even begin to comprehend.
In turn, had he been able to express it,
he would have found her narrow vowels quaint,
the shushed 's' when she said 'west' unearthly
and none of it as ladylike as she was trying to project.

Johnjo endured the repercussion
of a very bad crack on the head
when a soft-spoken boy of twelve.
Once studious and charming,
now his loves were startling rabbits
and yodelling at foxes and hares.
He would stand up and pull on the reins,
trying to screech to a sudden stop
on the curve of each and every bend,
as if he were the huntsman in charge
of a tireless pack of hounds,
imaginary horn to hand,
eager to report on the lie of the land.
But the shafts were strapped
to the harness of long-suffering Peggy
and she had years ago figured out
how not to let him break her stride.
She knew the way home,
and got them there as if her charioteer
were a mere gust of wind blown in from the side.

The Mentor

Grace Traynor, Governess to the three Fitzmaurice children.

One like so many who had not married,
Grace lost her fiancé to the mud of the Great War.
There was such a dearth, afterwards, of men,
best not to be greedy, she said,
and her father had dissipated his wealth
so she, as much a lady as her employer,
was left doubly without means upon his death.
Impoverished, though an equal
in every other respect,
it was thus she came to educating
and was treated by Lady Bella as befitted a friend.
At breakfast in the family dining room
whether in flamboyant silk kimono
or fashion-plate, bias-cut dress,
she was more the eccentric, free-living aunt,
than a dowdy, put-upon governess.

After they met, Grace gave Venetia books to read,
judging her utterly bereft
in the matter of Gaelic heritage.
She would not countenance a nursery maid
who did not share a love of literature
with her three boisterous charges.
Beginning with James Stephens' *Crock of Gold*,
she would work backwards, if called for,
until they found an appropriate starting point.

Her new protegée had a yen for fantasy
which might be exploited for the moment
and the children would enjoy it,
but she intended to wean her
onto more political works.
She would not have her linger
in naïve ethereality
when the secular state was subordinate
to the bigots of the majority faith
and their Protestant creed and way of life
in peril of being effaced.

The Meeting

Seánie Milligan, Head Groom at Ragnallstown Stud

Lithe and dark,
fit and handsome at thirty-eight,
his soul jumped when he saw her.
She proffered a distant hand,
lost amongst so many strangers.
He held it and fell
beyond his depth in those peridot eyes.

Johnjo, his eldest, was the outcome
of a couple of illicit years
with a girl whose licence had been exhilarating,
cowsheds in the wet, cocks of hay in the dry.
They were younger than Johnjo was now.
Then, while she was upstairs giving birth to their sixth,
her heart was deadened, her appetites brought to a halt
when her firstborn plunged, headlong and screaming,
from the beech at the bottom of the kitchen haggard.

His wife adduced guilt in her free-wheeling youth,
its logical cure in abstinence and prayer.
She withdrew to leave Seánie a husband in name,
father to six but otherwise celibate and forsworn.

The Fabulist

The Servants' Hall, Ragnallstown House.

That new girl had floated, insubstantial,
behind his eyes all day.
He had a sense of renewal,
as if his life could start up again, untainted,
though he knew in his straitened heart
that the chances he had felt
anything which could turn out to be
more than a moment of lunacy,
a joke brought on by hunger
and the crisp Autumn air,
were further than remote.
Another look would undeceive him
and then, chastened,
he might take his leave.

At dinner, he was desperate to hear her speak,
for a personality to inhabit the splendour
of that sylph-like physique,
but she was silent, eyes down,
until they brought in the dessert.
Then the housekeeper drew her in
to the general conversation.
She voiced little more than insubstantialities
but they came couched in such soft, melodic tones,
with so much unconscious grace
so beguiling a need to deflect attention from herself
that it made his heart sing.
Here was the matching of promise
with a reality he had steeled himself to hope for in vain.
He took himself off to the stables after dinner,
unable, for the time being, to go home.

Next morning, he met her as she descended the stairs,
stepped back to let her enter the servant's hall.
He knew that to her he was the head groom,
a rank equal to housekeeper.
He also knew he had been a father
for longer than she had been alive
and took this on the chin, without rancour.
He did not know he was the kind of fabulist
her piqued imagination had begun to require.

The Bridegroom

Dolly was in season,
Carraigboffin Belle in the stud book,
and her English suitor,
Daytonian Dangerous Dan,
was sulky and out of sorts.
He had one more day to do the deed
then he would be back again at sea,
another bout of equine *mal de mer*
his only recompense.

He had been tetchy
and she incensed by his brattish ire.
So far, no sign of congress
between these hunting aristocrats,
with more courtiers present
than ever verified
the deflowering of a nubile queen.
Then Seánie had a man-to-man word
in Danny Boy's roan ear.

It would not be the first time
he had coaxed a prince to shed his seed,
however undignified the public act,
and while it might have been the extra oats
the noble bridegroom had been served the night before,
the whispering knowhow of his *maître d'*
or simply Nature moving at her own implacable pace,
another thoroughbred foal was brought into being.

There was a yard-wide sigh of relief,
that is, until it was time to buckle up again
for the next dynastic mating.

9

The Celebration

That evening there was a feast,
a little extra with dinner,
porter for the men,
sweet sherry for the women.
Across the table they bandied,
male and female in the same vein,
lewd comments on Dangerous Dan
and his last-ditch swordsmanship.
Each coupling underwrote their livelihoods
to a degree that Vinnie,
their merriment demanding
a more approachable form of her name,
was too much the ingenue to guess.

What is more, absorbed in drink and ribaldry,
they failed to remark the tongue
of a softly-spoken, well-nigh silent man,
after years of introspection
suddenly let loose like the stallion's affections.
In words made clumsy from under use
and seated in an alcove near the stairs,
the head groom quietly spun a tale of the Fianna
to an audience of one:
the well-worn yarn of the doings of the court of Tara
when they came carousing down the hill at Bealbog,
the Gaelic name of the Fitzmaurice Ascendancy estate.

The Fianna

What happened was they came of a sudden one night, in the middle of a very hot Summer. They all traipsed over from Tara for no better reason than to see could they make as good a bonfire on the top of Bealbog as they could on the hill of Tara itself. They gathered up a whole load of yellowed weeds, twigs and dried leaves and set it alight. But what they didn't think of, while they were at it, was all the thick, dry furze on Bealbog and the state it would be in that Summer with not a drop of rain for weeks. And the whole place went up like a tinderbox, with a fire that burned for seven nights and seven days that could be seen for seven leagues in any direction. Well, they were fine and satisfied with it, and themselves, until the morning of the eighth day when they wanted to move on and couldn't because they weren't able to put out the blaze. They left it for another whole day and a night in the hope that something would change in their favour but nothing did and, shamefaced, they had to call in the druids. Now these were a nasty bunch and they didn't like anyone but themselves messing with fires on hilltops and besides that they had taken a strong set against the High King of the day. They thought he wasn't taking them or himself seriously enough and they were going to teach him a lesson. You see, they could have put out that fire at any time with one flash of their wands, but they didn't. They turned up instead on the ninth day with a plan. They told the king and all his court that if he didn't do what they said the fire would never be put out and it would spread throughout the whole country and then where would they all be. So he agreed, poor devil. On the evening of the ninth day, they stripped him naked, shaved every bristle of hair off his body with a piece of sharpened limestone, coated him from head to toe in green moss and lichen, rammed him into in a rough oak barrel, packed it with a load of stinking seaweed they had carted specially from the coast and then set it rolling all the way down the hill to where the land flattened out at the bottom. The fire quenched itself in all directions as the barrel rolled through it, they made sure of that, all the while with the High King yelping and squealing inside in it, and the court, not knowing whether to laugh or to cry, urging him on. Mind now, the gods were greater than the druids and they wanted them to know it. So when the king reached the bottom of the hill, everyone could see that a stream had sprouted where the barrel had passed and flowed down the hill as if it had always been there. The druids knew at once that this was the king's redress and a warning to them to keep clear of him ever after, which they did. The stream was known since then as Shrathancrur, Conor's Stream, and the High King in those times was the most famous of them all after Brian Ború, Conor MacNeasa. So now for you.

The Hill

The tale, had she known it,
coaxed into her consciousness by a man
who drew breath only to look at her,
sent her looking for a martial mound,
of which there was none,
only a knobbled eruption
on the monotonous rolling turf.
It boasted a meagre growth
of tawny, stunted gorse,
no stream ran through it,
only a landscaped copse
either side of a path
running down to the house.

The staggered wood,
limes to the front
and elms taller behind them,
exuded a cloister-like peace,
with a gentle swoosh
in the layering of leaves
as the breeze wound its way
through their translucent greens.
And then Seánie appeared.

There were twigs aplenty underfoot
but he made no sound.
In her reckoning, men and the land
were like Siamese twins
with a natural right
to be around each other.
She gave no thought
to being nonplussed.

The Walk

They were out for hours,
well beyond darkness
and any notions of decency,
she, rapt in the cloak of his imaginings,
he, aware of the sting in the tail
but too much in thrall
to the glamour of those fabled Gaels.

He had never told such yarns out loud before.
He would have been jeered into silence
for daring to recount a past that was not his
in vowels that betrayed his urban roots.
Though in the place of his birth
he might have become a different kind of raconteur,
a Dublin wit, like many tenement kids before him,
in the country he had had to restrict his remarks
to the bare practicalities
for his narrations would never pass muster
in the judgement of the locally born and bred.

For all those emigré years
he whispered his tales only to his beasts,
the more cantankerous and aloof the better,
and thus, when she bid him a distracted goodnight,
he melted away to the stables
to talk to his other beloved,
the imperious and newly-gravid Carraigboffin Belle.

The Confidante

Dolly was his favourite girl,
almost his best friend.
He had been there at her birth
and every other happening
in her pampered life,
more closely involved
than in anything to do
with his children or his wife.

Though haughty and temperamental,
the russet mare routinely soaked up
the weight of Seánie's workaday cares.
It was an article of their kinship
and they conversed in little nudges
and, on her side, snorts and sighs
to which his habitual responses
were minimally verbal.

Yet she was thrown
by his unaccustomed elation
and whickered her concern.
Somehow she understood
better than he wanted to himself
that this seeming gift,
finally, from the benevolent gods
brought the very opposite
of what he hoped it would.

In the meantime Venetia,
still afloat among the stars,
bumped into a worried housekeeper
as she ascended the back stairs.

The Perturbation

Katy Halpin, housekeeper.

'Holy Mother of God, child,
where were you out to until this hour of the night?
You put the heart crossways on the lot of us.
I'm only after saying that we were a bit worried
with you being new to the place
but with visitors to do with the horses upstairs
there was no-one I could send out.

Did you get any dinner at all?
Sure run down and tell cook
I said you could have a bite
of whatever is left over, she won't mind,
she's only just finishing up herself now.

That Shrathancrur copse is a devil in the dark,
I got lost there myself once.
It was only the luck of God
that brought me down on the right side
before the house was locked up,
or I'd have been a hobo for the rest of the night.

But sure, you're back, that's all that matters
and you're only young once.
Least said soonest mended.
Go on down to the kitchen Vinnie, pet,
and, sure, whatever it was you were up to,
it'll just be between yourself and myself.'

Venetia went to bed beneath her patchwork cover
to dream of Shrathancrur and all the Gaelic wonders
that seemed to her much so much more alive and true
than the stodgy tales doled out in Grace's serious tomes.

The Spouse

Úna Milligan, née McDermott.

No will o'the wisp wood sprite
but a flesh-and-blood man,
perilously attracted against his duty,
his custom, his demeanour,
went home in a daze to his wife.

Úna was on her knees
telling her habitual litany,
the austerity of a contemplative order
like a grille wall between them.

He blew out the lamp on his side
and attempted to cross the threshold into sleep.
If this marvel had no name,
there could be nothing of which to disapprove.

The Summer

By tacit agreement they met on Sundays in the lime grove
and he walked her over most of the humps and hollows,
hidey-holes and beauty spots of the estate,
all the while recounting tales, authentic and invented,
of the fairy creatures and famous heroes who had once dwelt there
and left traces of their being in the anglicised placenames.

She tried to reciprocate with artless versions
of what she had read in Grace's tomes, always clamouring to know
if this and that could have happened
and how they might have left their mark on the land if so.
Together they inhabited a different world,
one where his word was law, where his imagination dominated,
where his explanations were always right.
But the more he took stock of her questions,
the more he knew she could only be an honorary daughter,
an exquisite faery child, not even a foil like Dolly,
the materiel of womanhood somehow untraceable
behind the portals of those moss-green eyes.

It was only gradually that he began to comprehend
that he had managed to trap them in an excruciating bind.
If ever there was gossip, no quarter would be given,
they were blow-ins and disposable in the clannish local mind.

The Advocates

Grace Traynor, prosecution

'Venetia dear, you know that these stories are very important in the history of any nation and particularly for ours since we were dispossessed of them for so long, but you mustn't think of them as archaeology. They're as true as any set of folktales, which means probably not at all. Yes, there were high kings and druids, and scholars and saints, and tribes and Brehon Laws and all sorts of disputes over territory and rights, but they were not the kind of fantastic feats glorified in the tales of Fionn Mac Cumhaill or Cú Chulainn. The people who lived here in the centuries before St Patrick were as ordinary as you or I and their world wasn't all that different. It's just that it was the custom hundreds of years ago to make sense of all of this by dressing it up in magic. People were illiterate and that was how they could best remember. It was a long time before there was Christianity or science to help them put things in perspective. But we must try not to lose that sense of proportion ourselves, sweetheart, especially when we are in charge of the education of the young.'

Seánie Milligan, defence

'Well, Vinnie, science and Christianity, I don't know. You see, life has a way of showing a different face to each and every one of us, wouldn't you say, now? I mean, take my old pal, Dolly, she knows a power of things about this world that I'll never dream of, and she won't tell me because after all I'm only a human and I'll never be part of Mother Nature in the way she is, or any other animal walking God's earth for that matter. Our ancestors were a lot closer to the land than we are now. Electric light and motor cars and aeroplanes are putting an end to a lot of things the old people took for granted, and let's not even talk about factories and cities. God help us, I saw enough of them when I was a boy to last a lifetime, and none of it good, darlin' girl, none of it. Take the family we all work for here as an example. The Fitzmaurice name goes back to Norman times. Fitz means 'the illegitimate son of' and Maurice must have been some Norman knight or nobleman who came this way and fell in love with an Irish lady and had a son or maybe more children. It wasn't such a great thing in those days to have children without being married, it wouldn't always have been that easy to find a priest. But then, these people still had the old wisdom and they knew that what was in your heart was what truly mattered. So, here is a name that goes back almost a thousand years, to a very different kind of living, and those people, those Normans were the ones who came here and became more Irish than the Irish themselves. Now, there couldn't be a greater compliment than that, could there? Mind you, the lady who fell in love with the first Maurice was from one of the big families around here, the Ó Nualláins, going back to the time of the Fianna and Shrathancrur, and so the Fitzmaurice name was just a new way of continuing an old tradition. You see, that's what's gone wrong with the modern world. Everything is about what you can see and what you can make and what you can prove. But, sure the world couldn't be that simple or what would be the point of it? What would we be doing here if that's all it was? No, I'd say when Fionn and Oisín and Oscar walked the land and the Hound of Culann was the gatekeeper of the north, that was a time when humans lived to the full extent of what they could do. We lost that somewhere along the way, maybe when the Fitzmaurices began and the Ó Nualláins ended, and now we can only remember it, and maybe catch a glimpse of it now and again'.

Grace Traynor, prosecution

'I agree, of course, that the history of our placenames and family names is very important. The Fitzmaurice name unites Catholic and Protestant heritage and now above all this is something that we need to remember. And the Wallaces, your family, and the Traynors, mine, are just as much part of this nation as Katy's and Seánie's, the Halpins and the Milligans. In fact, this is certainly something we could explore more with the children. Thank you for bringing it up.'

Seánie Milligan, defence

'I'm sure you're right, Vinnie darlin'. I'm only a poor townie myself, however hard I try. Most of Dublin has British Empire street names anyway so it's hard to relate the old tales to the city, apart from the Hill of Howth of course, but that's a long way from the Liberties where I grew up. And, sure, God Almighty, can't I can see Dolly laughing away at me right now, as if to say this is what she always wanted an ignorant Dublin jackeen like myself to realise in the first place, how much closer we are to our past out here. You see, the fine tuning, the instinct, is not in my blood in the way it's in yours. It's a true gift you have, girl, and whatever else you do, don't ever let anybody, not even Grace Traynor, who's a grand woman in every other respect, talk you out of it.'

The Judgement

'Summary justice doesn't happen out of the blue',
so the parish priest said.
Johnjo was concussed, battered and in bed.
It was the last day of August,
the feast of the Apostle of the English.
Blithe, clumsy and curious,
he had tried to mount a little boy in the woods
on the way home from the Aidan's Day Fair,
an overdue reckoning
between his arrested child's mind
and the sap of a lusty young bear.
Not even those who had gelded calves and colts
had foreseen such a calamitous affair.

Úna was there
in the kitchen with the priest
and Seánie saw instantly
that there would be no way out.
She said nothing.
Long after the canon had gone
she kept a distance more profound
than all the years she had spent
beseeching a metal crucifix,
abject, on her knees.
She had been betrayed again by God,
and so acutely this time
that there could never again be words.

The canon's parting advice had been
'Look after your wife, there's a good man'.
Seánie knew his cross was now doubly weighted,
constant vigilance or the asylum for Johnjo,
more of the same or the grave for his wife.

The Farewell

No-one went quite so far as to suggest
that Johnjo would not have been in trouble
had his father spent his Sundays at home
instead of walking the country with a girl
young enough to be his daughter,
and she of the other faith as well.

Yet Rome and Canterbury met in synod
and decreed the innocent must leave
while the vaguely culpable
attended to both wife and child.

A glowing reference was produced,
the possibility of another position,
and Venetia left a few days later
seemingly oblivious of the father's burden,
the nature of the son's disgrace
or any hint of the whispered observation,
'a Protestant from the West,
what else could you expect?'

The Sentence

Her face had been continuously before him.
When he came across anything that seemed intriguing,
hers were the reactions uppermost in his mind.
He had begun to inhabit his life, the better part of it,
through the enthusiasms of that wide-eyed, faery child.

Now, in all the bitter clarity
of hindsight and catastrophe,
he saw how colourless his world had been for years
only to find his Indian Summer gone,
consumed in a sudden plume of smoke
and his stories caulked up
in a silence more complete
than the mutism he had endured before.

He had no way of saying goodbye
and watched her go without a solitary word.
From then on, only Dolly understood.

II

The Amazon,
Autumn and Winter 1940-1941

The Roost

In the family home,
her room had been no bigger
than a sizeable trunk,
improvised under the eaves
and not really big enough,
but she was the only girl
and she brought a homely touch
with dress-fabric remnants over a wooden box,
seashells, beach pebbles, quirky stones,
illustrations from ladies' magazines,
dried ferns and pine cones,
a minuscule washstand
with a rose-patterned jug
and a tarnished mirror that enshrined
those geometric cheek bones.

Too hot in the Summer,
too cold in the Winter,
it was nonetheless
the crucible of her early dreams
and in it she felt,
as nowhere else,
safe and fully at ease,
and never more so
than in the wake of her banishment
from the Fianna and the lime grove leaves.

The Rumours

Her brother's wedding, in early November,
was the highpoint of all speculation,
with tales being carried to every hole and corner
of her listlessness and lack of animation.

'Protestants and all, wouldn't you think
they'd pack her away somewhere
or find the blackguard who did this,
hold a shotgun to his balls
and make him marry her before it shows.'

Despite the anthem of the moment,
Venetia continued slender and in full view
long enough to scotch predictions
of seedy Midlands congress.
This left wagging tongues no option
in their all-consuming worry
but to diagnose a more traditional malady,
there being 'a bit of a want',
hadn't they always said it, in that lady.

The Metropolis

Proctor & Masters, Chemists, estd. 1897

January found her in London,
behind the counter of the chemist's
on her aunt Ethel's prosperous street,
still in the blue dress that had done
for the nursery at Ragnallstown
and some of her wandering with Seánie
through the Shrathancrur trees.

The pharmacist, Vernon,
was a 'confirmed bachelor',
admirers of all convictions holding hard
to the accepted euphemism
because he was revered for miles around
for diagnosis and cure
on a par with the best of Harley St.,
whose moneyed clients were
sometimes to be found
explaining their conditions
across the boxes of rose-violet creams
and *Echt Kölnisch Wasser*
on his cluttered mahogany counter.
He was also and perhaps astutely
an inveterate chatterbox.

Venetia listened for hours
to his chit-chat and prognostications
and by the end of her first year
she was almost as sharp as he was
when it came to symptoms and palliation.
She grew too to understand the full value
of prolonging conversation
and deployed it, with unassuming hesitancy,
when the master was not present,
to assess that moment's ailing patient.

When the Blitz began,
she volunteered to be an ARP warden
and astonished all who knew her
by coping as if to the city streets born.
As long as she had the armband on,
she went in fear of nothing,
dependable as any veteran of the trenches
and the fire brigade combined in one,
though not even she knew where that facility
could claim its origins from.

The Feat

Lucknow Cottages, East London.

Exhausted and far too few,
the firemen had failed to notice
the two girls trapped in the middle house.
Venetia came up the alley
behind the burning ends
of the butter-brick terrace
drawn by their shrieking.
The rear of the building was still intact
but there was smoke pouring out
through all the apertures on the bottom floor,
with the children at the window above,
screaming, fluttering,
unwilling to be tyro angels.

Not for the first time,
there was a convenient tree.
From there it was an easy reach
to the lean-to roof of the coal house,
the gradient not so steep she could not crouch
and lever up the wooden sash at the back.
In an instant, the girls drifted down
on a cloud of flannelette sheets in candy-stripe,
cherubs after all, but of the earthly kind.

Without stopping to catch their breath,
the three of them sauntered, devil may care,
around the gable corner
and into the gardened square,
at which point the little girls' dazed debonair
dissolved as they flew
to their distraught grandpa and nan.
Venetia skirted around the weeping huddle
and melted, much like the Shrathancrur druids,
into the heavy, cordite-infused air.

But the local paper was on the job,
and the children remembered
their saviour's unusual name.

The Cohort

Bert Morris and Mattie Haynes, retired welders.

She had patrol mates
who could not keep up with her,
a pair who had come through the Somme,
Mattie and Bert, still in their prime
but more fearful now
than they remembered being
in that older war.

'Vinnie, my girl, all joking apart,
you shouldn't take such risks,
it isn't right, a young girl like you,
you should leave all that to the fire brigade,
them lads are trained for it and you're not,
however much you get away with it.
I know there's a war on and all that,
but there's got to be some limits.'

'Bert is right, Vinnie, love,
don't do it again, for God's sake,
we don't want to have to put you in a box.'

'Still, Mattie and I was very proud of you,
we said so to that newspaper man
who came round just now.
We didn't think you'd mind.
They're going to put you in the paper.
They said it would be good for morale
and the Almighty Siddons is thrilled
to have his unit in the *Herald*.'

They would always stand behind
their elfin Atlantic foundling
even if theirs was never to comprehend,
so unperturbed on the surface,
so liable to take off
and do something sickeningly risky
at the drop of each and every bomb.

Their own daughters, of similar age,
were nursing infant children,
no more capable of Venetia's stunts
than of winning a National Hunt chase.
They thought it might be the Irish in her
but admitted the labouring Paddies
of their dockyard acquaintance
were nowhere near that crazed.
Bert opined it might be the confections
in that highfaluting chemist's shop,
but Mattie replied to the effect
that those same decoctions
were reputed to produce
the most salutary results
on just about everyone else.

And so, they carried on,
as they always had,
hoping her immortal kindred
would see fit to step in
if ever there was urgent need.

The Stupefaction

George Conway, reporter on the Herald.

Young and able but not in uniform,
childhood tuberculosis,
a scourge as yet unbeaten,
he carried no little guilt
but every so often
a small part of him would rejoice,
a socialist and a pacifist at heart.

He saw Venetia,
honed into something beyond beauty
by hazard and intensity.
The contact was as if with cool, unfathomable glass.

Bert and Mattie witnessed his stupefaction.
Romance might be a cure
though they held out little hope,
George was hardly the most dashing
of her brushed-off, would-be beaux
but they took a shine to him even so,
and egged him on
inviting him to come with them on patrol,
regaling him with tales
of her ladyship's derring-do.

'Well then, Bert, what was we about last night?'

'We went down Pennant Way,
where the old public toilets was closed down,
you remember, not deep enough for a shelter,
and too many hiccups with the sewerage
to keep them open.'

'Ah, yes, a terrible place when we was kids,
dirty old men and dirtier raincoats,
wouldn't like to say what went on there.'

'Careful, Mattie, young ears about.'

'Not this fine young man of the press,
dear Bertie, I hope?'

'Fair dues, old son and, after all,
he is obliged to report the truth.
Plus Vinnie just ignores us,
don't you love?
Her mind is on higher things,
George, most of them too lofty for us.'

'Never mind, Bert, I think he's gone.'

It had dawned on George
that she was entirely indifferent
to her corporeal splendour,
a wonder from which,
as he was brewing the tea,
he could not uncouple his eyes
nor distract his befuddled mind.

The *Fleur de Lys*

'Of course, fascism must be fought
but I sometimes think we're falling
into the hands of the worst type of capitalist,
but there is no way out, for now.
Who profits by this war?
Not the ordinary people bombed
by man-made thunder falling from the skies,
but the suppliers of uniforms,
tinned rations, parachutes, corned beef.
Can that be right? It all comes down
to trade and profit in the end.

There's a regular discussion at the *Fleur de Lys*.
There's one next week,
would you like to come along?
It perfectly above board,
we're all behind the war effort.
What do you say?'

She acquiesced,
as long as she could change her shift,
and suddenly he walked on air.
It was a long time, that night,
before he fell asleep.
In the midst of it all,
a little voice within him asked
if it could be right to be so joyful
in the midst of war.

The Stroll

They cut through Regent's Park in the half-light,
sheltered from the thoroughfares,
and took in the smells and sounds of the evening.
The sky was overcast and lowering,
a lull amid so much noise and combustion.
With little danger of a raid that night,
they ambled along and took their time.

She recounted the sundry exploits of her siblings
and the motley cats, dogs, hens, geese, chickens and ponies
who lived in symbiosis and occasional conflict
in the long garden-orchard at the back of their cottage.

To the son of Portsmouth shopkeepers
whose lives had always been dependent
on the ebb and flow of commerce on the quays
and who spent all his childhood on a cobbled street,
such existence was almost unimaginable:
the goose who nestled kittens under her wings
while the nursing queen was hunting vermin;
the dog who could tell who was at the door
and barked once for a child, twice for a woman,
three times for a man and four times for a pedlar;
the pony who put her head in the window every morning
for an apple, a carrot or whatever was going,
a working beast like Johnjo's Peggy,
twice as wise as any human she might meet.

Luminous eyes, an air of mystery
and a storybook existence such as this
would have turned the head of any mortal man
and he had no chance.
What was politics but a dull and lifeless thing
beside such glories?
He left her at the gate with an almost imperceptible bow,
noting in awe that the full arc of that gesture
would have meant kissing the back of her hand,
a slave to upper-class custom
after all that egalitarian talk at the *Fleur de Lys.*

He resolved to bring flowers the next time,
whatever he could manage to find.

The View

Vernon Masters, modern apothecary.

'Yes, well, of course
the press have to expose themselves
to everything in order to inform us.
He was only performing his duty, I'm sure.
I expect you were naturally curious,
under the circumstances, and perhaps
he's a nice young man, which is all well and good,
but still and all, this kind of debate
can be very dangerous.

I know we're fighting fascism
at the moment and that is a terrible creed,
built on grievous, grievous misunderstanding
of the Roman discipline and manner of running an empire,
but there are some kernels of truth there too,
about the way human nature must be organised
for its own benefit and good.
Communism, on the other hand,
is an appalling dogma, grinding everyone down
to the same atrocious poverty.
It's a dog-in-the-manger set of beliefs
whereby everyone must share in the same misery,
and, from what one can see,
it's become far worse than that in the Soviet Union,
worse than Czarist autocracy,
from the meagre amount of information
they allow to seep out and what one reads in the press.

The thing I cannot reconcile
is how ostensibly intelligent people
can look at the example of Russia
and think that Communism can be
anything other than an utter, abject failure.
And let's not even talk about that odious pact
Stalin, their so-called man of steel,
signed with that mountebank Hitler.

Vinnie, my love,
you can't possibly let any of this take hold of you,
it's a hideous, repulsive distortion.
Of what you ask?
Of Christianity of course,
the purest, truest respect
for the needs and wants of others.
The word commune
is the same as community
and a Christian community
is one in which everyone
is well provided for,
people are generous, open-hearted
and law-abiding.

That's the ideal, dearie,
and humanity is, I give you,
maybe the opposite of that:
without laws to regulate it
and police to enforce them,
flawed, deceiving, wretched.
Even very good people,
if left for long enough,
will give in to temptation,
if they think they can get away with it.
Man is an animal
and animals have to be trained and controlled,
otherwise they would trample all over us
and then we'd all be in a pretty state.
That's my view.'

ARP HEROINE SAVES THE DAY

by George Conway

Iris Drake, 7, and her sister Nancy, 5, were rescued from the flaming ruins of their house at No 11, Lucknow Cottages, Spitalfields last Friday by the intrepid action of ARP warden, Miss Venetia Wallace. Hearing the cries of the trapped children, Miss Wallace, with no thought for her own safety, climbed into the burning building and spirited the girls out through a first floor window just as the house was about to collapse around them. In a trice, she reunited the children with their distraught families and then modestly disappeared into the night.

Lest we forget, other houses and other children might be at risk only streets away and, for Miss Wallace, duty came first.

Young women, such as Miss Wallace, who carry out acts of bravery in these awful days as if there were nothing to it are an example to us all, to which end this newspaper sought Miss Wallace out, and went on patrol with her and her fellow wardens, Mr Herbert Morris and Mr Matthew Haynes, watching over this city as the dreadful rain of Luftwaffe bombs continues to blight us, night after night.

Continued on page 4.

Eastcheap Eagle and Hoxton Herald

Fearless Vinnie Fixit

darting like quicksilver through the flames

Bert and Mattie:

'You're famous now, Vinnie, they'll have you on the Pathé News next. We'll have to pay to see you in the picture house.'

George:

'So, what did you think? You don't think I overdid it? I mean, I hope it came across as a reasonable version of what you and Bert and Mattie have to cope with every evening.'

Vinnie Fixit II

Bert:

> 'Mind you, George, Vinnie's different, from the rest? Isn't she, Mattie? She's not like the wife, she don't complain or nag, she hardly talks. If it wasn't for them rescues of hers we'd barely know she was there at all, would we Mattie?'

Mattie:

> 'We wouldn't at that'.

Bert:

> 'So, where'd that leave the individual who was her husband, the poor blighter would never know whether he was coming or going tied to the likes of her'.

Mattie:

> 'You're right, mate, he wouldn't have a clue'.

Bert:

> 'And that wouldn't be the way to start a marriage, would it?'

Mattie:

> 'You can say that again'.

Bert:

> 'Now, George, old son, whose round is it?'

Vinnie Fixit III

Vernon:

'Ah, yes, you're Vinnie's young man, glad to make your acquaintance, very glad indeed.

You're not in uniform, I see, none of my business, of course. Oh, I'm sorry, tuberculosis, a very raw deal that and no mistake, well done for coming through with what looks like flying colours, if I may say so.

My sister's husband went that way, you know, unspeakably sad, they were only a couple of years married too. She's a telephonist in Whitehall now, something for the war effort, but far less dangerous I have to say than the scrapes Vinnie gets herself into.

Quite the Boadicea, that young lady, and here in the dispensary you'd never suspect she had such a martial side to her character.

Well, it takes all sorts and sometimes still waters do run deep.'

Vinnie Fixit IV

George's brother John:
> 'Hurry up, old man, I don't know what you're dithering about,
> there's a war on.'

> Had he met Venetia,
> he would not have been so gung ho.
> All the same, George asked to tag along again
> on their next patrol.

The Raid

They coaxed two old boys in a maisonette flat
to leave their beds for the air-raid shelter
and left their ninety-seven-year-old neighbour as she was
but remained by the fireside with her,
whereupon she took to flirting with George.

What might have been forward
were she a quarter of her age
and charmless in her middle years
bore the courtliness of times long gone.
If she herself were a mere slip of twenty
and not the guardian of a suitor's account
of that cavalry débâcle in distant Balaclava,
George would prove a close-run thing between them,
she gave Venetia to understand,
unlike the carnage of those horses and men.
Whence George, a stranger to poise at the best of times,
held himself erect, becoming the dashing dragoon
of that *grande dame*'s Victorian youth.
Vinnie should be proud of her fine young man,
she proclaimed with a tinge of chagrin,
in a cut-glass accent to boot,
and he feared he might there and then
blurt out the yearning of his bashful heart
but they had to leave to retrieve the two old men
when the all-clear siren began to hoot.

For them, the army had been an escape from the slums,
a way of seeing the world, earning a crust
and they told stories of the Zulu War and Khartoum.
Afterwards they came home
to build the houses that carpeted their part of London,
to settle down and forget what the Empire had promised,
and then defaulted on, when they were young,
but they pitied the conscripts in this new, machine-led war,
at least they had enlisted out of choice.
They never thought, when they were boys toiling in the desert,
that war would engulf them twice in their childhood home
and wondered if there was any point in trying to survive all of this
when it was so very difficult to envisage any future hope.

As they leant on him, George replied
it would be as well to do their best even so.
Would it not it be better to wait to see the world
they had given so much, in their heyday, to protect
at peace once more before they upped and left?

The Dream

Now that even the timorous began to feel their way
back to their houses in the small of the night,
George felt he could take the time to look up above.
The sky was about to unfurl again,
the dark lifting back like the lid of an oyster.
He thought it betokened happiness ahead,
ordained for him by the omens on high.

He had witnessed the triumph
of those three ancient survivors
and drawn strength from their testimony.
He understood too
the obligation to take the torch and run with it,
knew that he must marry while he could,
propagate while he could,
make his mark while he could
and now was surely his opportunity.
He would ask her to be his partner
for the days and years to come,
to endure nights like this while they lasted
and the settled life that must certainly be theirs
when all of this had died down,
should they have the fortune to survive
and exit on the winning side.

While they were still
streets away from the end of the patrol,
his heart raced and he could feel paralysis rising.
Even though words were his trade
and he could talk politics for hours on end,
he had no intimate eloquence
in which to express himself.
He found facts and emotions
could exist a long way apart
and on that latter terrain
he became easily dismayed.
Now, anything he thought of
grew jumbled and incoherent
in the short gap
between his mind and his tongue.
He would find nothing to say
when they were finally off duty and alone.
The terror, the abyss had become too great
and, in any case, she would reject him,
or worse, pretend not to hear
in order not to offend.

So then the questions began.
Who did he think he was
to merit this creature of paradise?
That is why Bert and Mattie,
even Vernon, ignored him,
they knew already
and did not want to make it worse.
He grew alienated, anchorless,
on the point of sheering away,
onto a safer goodnight.
Then he thought of the flirtatious old lady
and the glint in her eye.
If she had not seen something,
would she have teased them?
He might not be deluded after all.
He must go on and do it now.

As they crossed through Hallows Oak Green
he begged her to sit for a while
to look at the dawn.
His legs would hold him no longer
and his breath was getting very short.
Had he hurt himself
in some way she had not noticed?
Had helping the old men been too much?
He said no, too panicked to be cross
that she invoked his tuberculosis,
and they sat there in silence.

When he recovered,
he said he had something to ask her.
She turned away from her reverie
to find out what the matter was
and, as the colour in those peridot eyes
rose and grew limpid with the sun,
his fear disappeared,
and with it his inarticulacy.

The Excursion

It had been a bright and crisp Winter Sunday,
they saw the pale sunlight
on the remaining shards of glass in Coventry cathedral,
imagined Godiva on her white palfrey
riding along the still discernible medieval streets,
once a place of church bells, oak-beamed pie shops
and taverns playing host to Crusaders.
Evensong near the cathedral, tea in a café just across,
and, from George, companionable talk,
of which there was likely a bit too much.

History and Politics:
    'Angles and Saxons,
    then the Normans
    and all the trouble
    over allegiances and language.
    Godiva was a Saxon lady,
    the cathedral is a Norman edifice,
    no-one cares any more
    as long as the factories produce,
    as long as the work gets done.
    But these are Angles and Saxons
    threatening us again.
    Hengest and Horsa then,
    but they still want *Lebensraum*.
    What if we gave in to them?
    Would it matter in a hundred years?
    People just got on with things
    and then the Normans came.
    Maybe the French will return
    in the new millennium
    and dispossess them,
    if that's how it ends.'

Religion and Gargoyles:
    'Do I believe in Hell?
    You mean do I believe in one
    populated by the likes of them,
    those nightmare visions up there?
    It's easy to frighten children with those ideas,
    but I'm not sure.
    There is such a thing as goodness,
    it's not evenly distributed,
    and beauty has to come into it some way.
    I mean beauty inside,
    that must come from somewhere,
    maybe that kind of beauty
    is a sort of reminder of a higher power
    or an overarching something
    there for us to glance off, occasionally.

    The bad stuff?
    The Manichean universe, you mean?
    I don't want to believe in that
    though it's very hard not to at the moment.
    I wouldn't say there's a creature called the Devil
    down here orchestrating the whole thing.
    We don't need supreme beings for evil to exist.
    Oh Lord, I've just said the opposite
    about goodness and beauty, haven't I?
    Let's have tea, I'm tied up in knots,
    hoist on my own petard,
    you might say, in Shakespeare's backyard.'

    They had tea, caught the train home,
    kissed (oh glory!), not too awkwardly,
    at Ethel's garden gate,
    then slept in their separate, blameless beds.

The Green

In that neat little square
at eight o'clock in the morning,
the January sun just upon the horizon,
with passion, vehemence and sweet reason,
he proposed.

It should have been his finest moment.
He had gathered all his being unto himself
in that single, simple request,
but he was never to hear her reply,
nor even see one register in those grassy-hued eyes.

In the instant it would have taken her to utter
that most dreaded or desired riposte
they were flung fifty yards apart,
landing on opposite edges of the small, frosted lawn,
recognisable as themselves, as human beings,
but only intuitively so.

A bomb from Hamburg
that had lurked a month or more
in the bole of the age-old Hallows Oak
lurched infinitesimally that night,
enough for it to erupt
and tear George's dreams
and his body asunder.
All the undertaker could do
was render him presentable
for mourning by his family.

She received a telegram from the king,
the best orthopaedic care
her battered local hospital could provide
and advice she must never again
be under significant physical strain.
Grateful for her survival,
her parents decided the only answer
was a return home to them in the West.

A Letter from Ethel

Dear Gert,

I know what you mean about Vinnie not talking to you. We didn't get anything out of Freddie either. I don't mean that he wasn't his usual jolly self, but he simply would not talk about being shot down. He lost a lot of his friends and he won't talk about that either. This stiff upper lip business is important, I do understand, but I don't think it's really all that healthy. You're lucky over there in that lush Irish paradise you married into that you don't have to pretend all the time. Anyhow, for the moment I know I should be glad he's alive.

In answer to your question, I don't have any definite idea of what Vinnie's understanding with poor George Conway was. I can see that the local gossip must be very annoying, but funny too, you must admit, all that stuff about her being engaged to a duke and so on. He seemed such a nice young man, no sides to him at all. She never said anything to us about what was going on. I do feel for his parents. They nearly lost him when he was fourteen. He was in a sanatorium for a whole year and it was touch and go for the first couple of months. I can't imagine what it must be like for them to lose him like that. I thought only Charles Stuart hid in hollow oaks. That's probably in very bad taste, but we must laugh.

Her ARP mates, two wise-cracking old codgers, came to the boat train to see her off. They drop round occasionally now as well for news of her. So she left her mark.

I'll miss her myself. She kept me company when everyone else was away. She isn't like anyone in our stolid Kentish clan. Is there anyone on Ted's side like her? A Celtic mystery somewhere along the lines? She was very popular with Vernon's customers and all. They said she had a healing touch (another surprise?) and that doesn't grow on trees – sorry, appalling pun in the circumstances – but you know me …

Your loving sister,

Eth.

A Reference from Vernon

Miss Venetia Wallace was in my employ as a pharmacist's assistant for two years. When she took up her post, on the highest references from people of repute and standing in her own nation and in this city, she quickly showed herself mistress of all her responsibilities. She exercised great tact, consideration and no small amount of flair in dealing with customers, many of whom were in severe distress and in need as much of counsel as the dispensing of drugs. I may say that I have some little reputation myself in the diagnosis of illness and Miss Wallace showed such sensitivity and awareness when assisting customers that I began to discern in her something of the same aptitude.

She was a responsible and dependable employee and never missed a day at work, in spite of her obligations as an ARP warden in the evening and at night. I have been very heartened to hear that she has made a full recovery from her dreadful misfortune.

She is a fine young woman of spotless character...

A Commendation from the Almighty Siddons

Miss Venetia Wallace, known in the press as 'Fearless Vinnie Fixit', served under my authority for seven months. In that time she, single-handedly and at considerable personal risk, pulled off a number of spectacular rescues, certain of which were reported in the local and national newspapers.

While it is undeniable that she persistently took inadvisable risks in her efforts to save lives, she came through each such endeavour with her own life and the lives of those she delivered intact.

Miss Wallace has made a signal contribution to the war effort, of which her family and friends may justifiably be proud ...

A Note from Bert and Mattie

Bert and me thought we'd drop you a little line just to see how you were. Never let them Nazis and their tricksy bombs get you down, not our Fearless Vinnie. If you don't mind us saying so, we don't think George would want you to give in either. We're delighted you're on your feet again.

There must be some old dispensary over there that could use your smile, even if there aren't any Jerry bombs to dodge. You was the best, love, we won't have another woman on our patrol after you, nor no lanky journalists neither, not after poor George, God rest his soul.

We've had a quiet time of it since you left. The Hun's run out of ammunition, maybe? Fat chance. Whatever happens, take care, love and don't forget your old pals …

The Correspondence

They never saw her again
but Bert and Mattie were assiduous
and their letters continued for years,
until Mattie, the letter-writer, died.

In all that time
Bert had been the talker,
the one who dictated most
of what was put on paper,
but with his sidekick dead
he had no heart to carry on.

He got his daughter to write once
to tell her of Mattie's death
and that was the end.

III

The Enigma, 1944-1945

The Offer

Sheathed in pearls and pre-war crêpe de chine,
Grace Trayor swept unannounced through the door,
sat down as if she had only been there the previous week
though she had been to visit just a couple of times before
and it was two years since Venetia had returned from her war.

That first time, she opened, in habitual languid tones:
'Venetia, darling girl,
I hear you're a perfect legend over there in London,
'Fearless Vinnie Fixit', they tell me. Well, well, well.'
Her mother produced tea and discreetly withdrew
as Grace threw off her fox-fur tippet,
took in the crutches and the invalid's blanket
and settled in to chat with her former protegée.
'A war heroine and practically a war widow
at one and the same time,
I was so sorry to hear your news.'
Though she had lost her own prospects
in not dissimilar fashion,
time and temperament had kept Grace sanguine:
'Memories are useful at this point.
I would cherish them if I were you', she enjoined.

For all her assurance and glamour
and all that she belonged to the self-same caste
as the Ascendancy families among whom she lived,
Grace was no more than hired help herself
and Venetia's dismissal from Ragnallstown
had rankled since the day it occurred.
Now, on this latest foray, she was finally in a position
to offer her young comrade suitable redress:
'A little bird told me you were looking for a post.'

'Hanorah and Helena Hassett,
they would be in their seventies or eighties now,
though you wouldn't know it.
The house is on the banks of the Shannon,
the other side from here,
but you would still be able to see home on a clear day.
It's a fine old mansion, with a big rose garden
and French windows all over the place.
Norah and Nellie aren't what you might call great readers,
they prefer their roses and walking the dogs
but they have a family library in need of a lot of attention.'

Their great-grandfather had financed
and housed a grand, multilingual library
and they venerated his memory, if not his many volumes.
Now that they were the last of the line
they wanted to bequeath his collection to the fledgling nation
but on their own terms and put in order first
by someone whose human qualities they could trust.
The position would be available
at the start of the following year.

When Venetia claimed ignorance and demurred
Grace was ready and outflanked her objections with ease:
'Your war record will appeal to them
more than the expertise you don't yet have.
When you get to know the ladies, you'll understand.
They're Catholics, by the way,
just in case I might have convinced you
all landed families had to be Protestants like us.'

The Arrival

Séamas Doherty, hackney driver.

'It's hard on a man whose only daughter saved up from her job over in Boston so he could purchase such a motor, cash on the nail, to see the same item in the hands of them army hooligans who wouldn't know a good automobile from a sack of onions. Emergency requisition my foot.

Oh, you should see the state she's in now, all scratched and bumped. Officers how are you, they're no better than jumped up good-for-nothings who never had a decent thing in their lives, the way they've no respect for quality when it's right under their noses.

If Imelda only knew what's been done to the poor, misfortunate Morris, she'd have forty fits. She writes and asks me how I'm getting on with the shortages and all and I do be beside myself trying to think of things to say that wouldn't be outright lies. Mind, the wife says 'tis only jealousy made them Army boys take the car off me in the first place. Mikey Corrigan, up the way, still has his Ford, and she says they left it to him because it was an old yoke from the twenties.

Still, the petrol rationing would probably have put a stop to my gallop anyway. At least poor old Jessie here doesn't need coupons to keep going. Wasn't she the fine, generous-minded beast, when all is said and done, to come back under the trap again after a couple of years minding her own business out in the field when the Morris was on the go!

As long as they don't start rationing the oats and the hay on us, we'll be grand I suppose, and, sure, we've no headlights on this contraption anyway to be seen by them Germans in the dark. So maybe things aren't all to the bad in the heel of the hunt.'

The Library

The tomes,
behind four windowed exits onto the sloping, lawned garden,

assembled
to furnish the stuccoed, single-storey, south-facing wing,

paid for
by barrels dispatched along the Douro in the time of Napoleon,

selected
to welcome a *fidalga* with three Iberian tongues and four family names;

a salon
decorated by sons of Bologna with quills, manuscripts and scrolls,

for a bride,
Maria Amalia Mendes da Silva Mendoza e Perelló,

reborn
as Molly, Mrs Malachy Hassett in the re-modelled Mount St James.

The Sentry

Josie Dalton, housekeeper.

The door was answered by an angular-looking creature in a dull green dress, very tall yet permanently stooped, like a heron who might miss something from her great height. Séamas made no attempt to acknowledge her and instead called out into the house.

'Miss Norah, Miss Nellie, the young lady is here.'

Josephine's tongue, on the instant, uncoiled with deadly intent.

'Who do you think you are roaring at the front door like a like a mangy old donkey after his feed and young Miss Wallace stood out there beside the trap? Have you no manners at all on you? The Lord between us and all harm, you'll have that misfortunate young girl out there thinking she's been dropped off in a lunatic asylum instead of a nice respectable house with two ladies known for miles around for their kindness and hospitality. Get yourself away out of that now Séamas, out of my sight.'

'Josie Dalton, you always did have a tongue on you that would scald the heart of a saint. Is it any wonder I won't converse with you when all I get is abuse no matter what I do or say?'

'Oh, 'twas the bad day they ever let any sister of mine take up with the likes of you. When I think of all the men lining up on the step and she had to set her cap at you. What are you? A hackney carriage driver without a shilling to your name if your daughter over in America didn't take pity and send the few dollars every so often to keep you from the poor house. My misfortunate sister, God be good to her, only the Lord Himself knows what led her astray.'

'Your sister married the best man for miles around and 'tis well you know it. What's more 'tis an awful pity you didn't follow her fine example yourself. It might have taken the edge off your tongue.'

'What? Tie myself up to the likes of you day in day out for the rest of my life, watching you drunk of a Saturday night after your fill of porter and then all meek and mild at the altar rails the following Sunday as if butter wouldn't melt in your hypocrite's mouth? I'd rather scrub floors in a cowshed than wash up after the likes of you.'

'Ah, now Josie, look, we've a job to attend to here. Shut up your old blather for a minute and give us a hand to help Miss Wallace in.'

Josie relaxed into a crooked half-smile and Séamas let off a guffaw.

'Right you are.'

The Ladies

A curious air of almost masculine authority,
big-boned, statuesque,
erectness and strength in their carriage
belying their nearly eighty years,
the square jaw and full lips of Greek antiquity,
voices with depth and sonority,
stentorian in their prime,
they were doyennes of all they surveyed.

The library, symmetrical on the surface,
but books shelved with neither reason nor rhyme,
the most recent and principal culprit being Josie,
sworn enemy of dust, cobwebs and all other signs
of things lying recumbent for too long;
Josie, who boasted
of never having read a book in her life,
would not let the volumes sit
for more than a week at a time,
though truth to be told, there was more to her rigour
than met the undiscerning eye.

The ladies had rejoiced
the day their governess left
and their father declared an end to their education.
They were meant to marry
but there was a dearth of suitable matches
and they had no mind to travel
in search of Catholic gentry husbands.
So they remained on the riverside mount,
made a profit from the orchard and the kitchen garden,
played bridge, held tennis parties,
walked their spaniels, rode to hounds.
From bustle to hobble and drop-waist to wartime utility,
one fashion had followed another
without the ladies much altering,
but now with their eyesight and energy fading,
they knew it was time to sort certain matters out.

The Monsignor

Nellie:

'The only person in the vicinity who pays any attention to the books, Miss Wallace, is Monsignor Davouren D'Arcy. He rather diplomatically reminded us of the value of Malachy's library and our obligation to do something about it. Without him, I dare say, you would not be here.'

Norah:

'It's odd, darling, you don't look at all bookish, more the dreamy type, I should say. Even so, you can never tell these days. When we were young you could tell so much more easily who was who and what was what. It's these short dresses I expect, they confuse everything. We would have called a girl who knew anything about books a bluestocking and you, my dear, don't fit the bill at all.'

Nellie:

'What my sister means, Venetia, is that you're far too attractive, if you'll allow me to say so, to fit into that old mould. But we're a long way off the fashion now and perhaps times have moved on without us. You see, Norah and I really only know about gardening, dogs and horses. We're very up-to-date on the latest horticultural fashions and we know good shanks when we see them. I'm not sure we can be trusted on much else though.'

Norah:

'Monsignor Davouren D'Arcy will probably come up tomorrow to make your acquaintance, as they say. He will give you instructions as to how you should begin your work. Nellie and I felt that it would be best that way. He knows as much about books as we do about roses.'

Nellie:

'I think you mean he knows a lot more, Norah dear.'

The Expectation

Every year, Venetia and her mother
remained in their pew
when the most freshly-ordained Redemptorist,
weak at the knees but keen to impress,
swore from the pulpit that all black Protestants
would, deservedly, rot in Hell.

As a result, she regarded Catholicism
as a less refined kind of faith,
consistent with foulmouthed horseplay
late at night on the village square,
though she and her mother were always welcomed
at the *grand guignol* of the annual Mission
and mixed comfortably with their neighbours there.

The monsignor did not look
like the usual, rough-hewn farmer's son,
choked in a celluloid collar,
awkward in a pleated soutane.
He came in an ordinary black suit,
an oblong of white at the neck,
with a folded umbrella
and a smart homburg hat.

Aubrey was a friend of the family
from childhood no less,
that winsome smile,
those see-through excuses for tearaway scrapes
all pickled in aspic now
as the sisters feigned deference
for the monsignor encased in his cloth,
his boyhood adventures mothballed
by the adolescent's unexpected choice.

Rome had sent him as diocesan secretary
to an incumbent who hectored money at will
out of tight-fisted farmers, beady-eyed traders,
the desperate and the credulous, rich or poor,
but whose uncouth manner offended
even the old women who knelt before statues
telling their rosaries hour after hour.
Fastidious amid the sleaze of Vatican City,
he had returned to a wave of hostility
from envious, less polished *confrères*
who vowed that over their dead bodies
'and the suffering soul in Purgatory
of every Catholic who had worshipped
at a rock out in a crag
or learnt their tables sitting on a ditch'
would a man of his entitlement
find advancement at home.

It was Grace who briefed him on the Fearless Vinnie
and what she had lost at the Hallowed Oak.
As he had time on his hands,
he welcomed the request.
Malachy's collection was an heirloom
he had long considered worthy of conservation.
He would be honoured to help bestow it on the State.

The Detection

Josie had turned down more than one proposal
so as not to leave her ladies in the lurch
though, if her suitors had been more prepossessing
or somewhat better off,
she might indeed have relinquished
what became her dogged lifetime's work.
What is more, while resolutely incurious
as to what lay between the card of each grand cover,
she had no desire for Malachy's gilded tomes
to leave his Babel of a library
for she wallowed in their ancient odours,
the fustiness of marbled paper and embossed leather,
and dusted and re-shelved a discreet few each week
in order to debauch her otherwise ascetic self.

And thus it was in their defence
she mounted her first sally.
It might prove to be a long crusade,
since no stranger, no matter how well-recommended,
would tread on hallowed Hassett turf
without Josie's thoroughgoing investigation.

She began with the new girl's dressing table,
on which stood an array of potions
she had never beheld in the town of Tourmascanlon,
nor even on the one trip she had made to the capital.
They were laid out beside a silver-backed vanity set
and a wedding photograph in a matching frame,
of Miss Wallace's blameless parents, no doubt,
young and hopeful in the standard, stilted, studio pose.

She saw nothing either to find fault with
in her underwear or her other clothes,
worn and out of fashion but kept in good repair
while her stockings and lace-up walking brogues
were equally beyond reproach.
Yet there was a pair of sandals, cream,
with tassels and a medium-height wedged heel
that seemed too risqué for a Catholic gentry home,
especially as they might pass before the gaze
of a consecrated bishop's secretary,
and Protestants, it was well known,
were not particular like the rest of us,
since they had married clergy.

She was perplexed moreover
to find no evidence
of bookish obsession on Venetia's part:
nothing learned or obscure,
no love of the objects in themselves;
no journal, no anthologies,
nothing precious at the bottom
of any of the drawers,
no dog-eared volumes, much-perused,
only a couple of ladies' magazines,
deeply unnerving as a cache
for the custodian of Malachy's calf-bound wealth.

How could it be that such a chit
could manage all this multiplicity of print,
which she herself could barely comprehend?
There was one decision only to be made.
She would have to trust her native wit
and, if one day out leapt
some snide unwholesome threat,
she would be the stalwart one to run to ground
the mischief at the heart of all of this.

The Pronouncement

The diocese of Kilcolman, four months before.

The Tuesday before the All-Ireland
the bishop was heard to say
that hurling was the Devil's work
because it kept good Christians
from thinking on the Word of God
at Mass of a Sabbath Day.
He did not mean it,
a dyed-in-the-wool enthusiast himself,
he let his tongue get ahead of him,
not for the first time,
and while it was disaster enough
that he should say it at all,
this was the year when the county team
was in Croke Park for the championship final,
after a wait of forty long years,
and the whole place was up in arms.

Afterwards, he went off to play golf
with no sense of the outrage he had caused
and, being the wildest, most erratic shot
that side of the Shannon,
no journalist would pursue him there,
knowing the likelihood
of having his head knocked off
by a sportsman who had never once
deigned to shout out the warning cry of 'fore'.

This was the incident that decided Aubrey's fate.
A bishop could not derogate
the secular gods of his rural congregation
and remain wholly unscathed.
Yet, to the hierarchy's outraged distaste,
Aubrey was dispatched by the Curia in Rome,
in reproof for their failure to ameliorate
Bishop Cahill's wayward tongue,
and, as they could not formally object
to a mere secretarial appointment,
they had to swallow their pride
and hope that biding their time
would eventually produce a dividend.
To which end, they side-lined him
in every conceivable way
and this left the monsignor with copious hours
for the cerebral pursuits
that beguiled him for so long
in pre-war Rome.

The Lesson

Monsignor Davouren D'Arcy sugars the pill.

'Do you know, Miss Wallace,
when I was a boy I came in here once
and worked out the number of books in this library.
I counted all the books on one shelf,
all the way across the back wall,
and found four hundred,
then I counted the number of shelves
and found eight,
that was three thousand two hundred books.
I calculated that the side walls were
about half the length of the back
so I allowed them sixteen hundred each,
the same for the garden wall,
since the French windows
and the rosewood cabinets
break the continuity of the stacks.
A grand total of eight thousand,
and that's only if you measure in folio volumes,
not to speak of the journals and pamphlets
in the various document drawers.
It was an overwhelming galaxy of objects
for a nine-year-old to contemplate,
and do you know what,
nearly thirty years later, it still is.

Now, if you look around this room
with the long leather spines and the soft light,
you would never think there were that many,
and each with its own story to reveal,
not just what's in them but where they came from
and how they made their way here as well.
A few hundred you might have said
if I'd asked you to guess
and you'd have thought you were...'

He stopped there.
She was young and unschooled
and he heard himself strike a patronising note.
The only way to row it back was with humour
and it felt maladroit, never his best suit.

'What we've actually got here is an unruly band
of what might kindly be called cherubs
who don't speak each other's language,
ducking and diving from hole to corner,
kicking and screaming and pulling each other's hair.
Getting them to behave like grown-ups
is the almighty task ahead of you here.'

Then he explained what cataloguing
such a number for the National Library
would really entail.

The Perambulation

Her back to the light from a French window,
heaped books on the desk in front of her,
all he could see was a shadowed oval
framed in a halo of coppery light.
As she rose from her chair to greet him,
those eyes emerged from the haze.
Madonnas in Italian galleries
with faces of unguarded innocence,
as if they had never given birth
or known what it was to suffer,
had the same placidity of gaze.
It had been weeks now
and still he could not reconcile
the dryad in the sunlit library
with what he knew of her Amazon past.

He had developed the custom
of taking her for the odd post-prandial walk,
a convenient means of instruction,
or so he thought.
He had begun with her education,
finding out what she knew,
what he could teach her,
whether she had a mind worth improving,
whether she would accept it if so.

That she was Protestant
made no difference to him
but it was politic to bruit abroad
that these promenades
might be means towards her conversion
to the One True Church.
Consecrated manhood he took as absolute
and, unlike many of his seeming pious brethren,
he did not believe himself sanctioned
by the sacrifice of the sacerdotal bind
to taste the bounty of the flesh while in vigour
only to recant and be forgiven
in the impotence of old age
or the face of untimely death,
though neither had he had eschewed
the platonic company of the opposite sex.
At least while in Rome,
where such interaction was easier,
he found unabashed pleasure
in greeting and taking leave like a civilian,
with a kiss on either cheek
for those whose intellectual company
he liked to keep.

This rendered celibate life negotiable
and he had emerged so far
with his heart and his vows unbreached.
He suspected, all the same,
that this plain sailing to date
may have had more to do with luck than address,
and that now he might be faced
with waters he determined to traverse
only if there were no other way through.
He could take refuge in ambivalence
as things presently stood,
though this was indulging in sophistry
and he could sense the stigma of betrayal beneath.

Not a man to waste finite time,
he had his calls down to the art of turning up
only when the weather would allow
some measure of outdoor pursuits
and he always brought some delicacy
that would appeal to Nellie and Norah
in lieu of what he fully understood to be
his duty to his long-time friends.
Though they rejoiced to find, once more,
some touches of the frolicsome boy
in the studious, cosmopolitan monsignor,
they fretted over the risk they feared was afoot.
As they saw no mischief in Venetia,
if there was jeopardy, it was bound to be his,
though Josie, for her part,
watched these jaunts with uneasy suspicion
and, in her case, the problem would always be laid
at the feet of that sandal-wearing chit of a Prod.

The Obligation

Each Winter Norah and Nellie became a little slower,
a little less alert to the doings of the outside world.
Josie felt acutely the diminution in tempo,
remembering the days when they were in their fifties
and she a slip of a thing barely out of her teens,
when they would walk five miles and back in a day
if they heard there was a rare plant to be seen,
a new foal or bull or a litter of pups,
not hearing of any mode of transport
beyond their own two feet,
as paired down in their devotion to husbandry
as any farming nuns behind a convent grille.

While the sisters rested after lunch,
Venetia and the monsignor dealt in the currency
of the agonised external world,
or rather he propounded and she occasionally replied,
mostly just umming and nodding her head.
George and Vernon talked a lot of politics in London
but most had thought no further than the next Luftwaffe raid
and taking advantage of the time in-between.
Now she began to see that at Mount St James
reflection was not a luxury but an obligation,
a kind of minimal tax levied on those not at the front.

When the war came, unthinking,
she followed what everyone else did.
She had no practical training
so they made her an ARP warden
with fire prevention and basic first aid.
They gave her a patch and a rota, and that was it.
She had no choice but to assume the burden
of the city in which she lived.
If she had been elsewhere, across the divide,
she would have done the same
as an ordinary person on the other side.

To Aubrey her stance had cast-iron integrity.
While politically simplistic, even naïve,
this must be how it was
for those with motherland roots and religion
in a secessionist state
but a foreign 'lilt' in the metropolis at war.
She had to be seen to be willing and useful
but otherwise disengage.

The Observation

The day came, on one of their walks,
when Venetia went as far
as to utter an adage
and did so as if she was the shaman
who had grasped it for the very first time:
your path was laid out for you
and could not be changed.

Aubrey was somewhat taken aback,
not just because she finally produced
what might be termed a contribution
to what had up to then been one-way traffic
but because the sentiment jarred
with her still tender age,
not to speak of his Thomist training
and humanist persuasion,
and so he felt obliged to enquire:
'Then why make any decisions,
big or small,
if your life is a voyage
in which you go where the ship takes you,
without ever being able to stop it,
steer it or get off it at all?'
The only response he got
was an inward smile,
an intimation of knowledge innate
and not, like his theology, acquired.

Indeed, until of late,
he had taken her intelligence to be
a gauzy, honey-toned glade,
delicate and obliquely lit,
without much focus or organisation,
wherein the discipline of reason
could be only introduced
using the most sensitive approach.
Now he was beginning to doubt
that any such transformation
should ever be assayed.

When the cataloguing was over,
he would go to Dublin more frequently,
spend more time in the National Library,
become again what was required of him,
scholarly and studious of habit.
He might also go to the races once in a while,
place the occasional clerical bet.
As a student, his luck had been prodigious
and it had not deserted him in his ordained years.
A judiciously-placed half-crown
recouped ten shillings or more,
no matter where or when he tested the going,
no matter how long it was since his last flutter,
nor how blasé he had grown.
Never having been in thrall to fortune
nor losing a wager,
such fragilities were, to him, unknown.

The Return

Séamas:

'I'm beginning to think I'm just as well off without the old Morris anyway. Sure, you can't talk to a motor vehicle when you'd be on the road on your own with nothing else to do and Jessie here understands my every word. We've a partnership going back years, years, faith, and she never held it against me for one minute when I let Imelda get me the old car, now what do you think of that? Aren't the animals a shining example to us all when everything is said and done?'

Josie:

'Wipe your boots, Séamas Doherty, if you mean to carry Miss Venetia's bags up to her room. I only spent the most of this morning polishing the hall floor and I didn't do it so the likes of you could come in and muck it all up on me. Are all men gligareens or what? I declare, the only man coming into this house who knows the value of floor polish is the monsignor himself and that's because he lived for years in them foreign places where you could eat your dinner off the marble floors. The Lord knows, if you tried to eat anything off the floors around here, with all the respect I get, you'd be poisoned before the bite of food even got as far as your gullet.'

Séamas:

'Ah, would you listen to her, Miss Venetia, as if I didn't know how much the monsignor butters her up and tells her she keeps this old place as well as the Pope's own housekeepers in Rome, nuns the lot of them.'

Josie:

'Give over, Séamas, you know as well as I do he has better things to do. Now, you can go on out there to the kitchen once you've done the bags. 'Tis a fierce cold evening and there'll be a bit of dinner out there on top of a pot for you. Yours will be served in the dining-room, Miss Venetia. Welcome back, I hope you had an enjoyable Christmas at home.'

The Catalogue

The catalogue was almost complete.
Venetia was to travel to Dublin to meet the librarian
with the monsignor there to settle the sisters' bequest,
his gravitas indispensable to the transaction.
She had listed the books according to tongue,
of which there was a plethora, ancient and modern,
for which Aubrey provided title translations;
then topic and publication date,
reasonable for a private collection
but for presentation to the National Library,
a matter of no little sisterly debate,
though at this late stage
it boiled down to the matter of boxing the volumes
in tens or twelves in the various crates.

Nellie:
    'Ten seems a much more familiar figure:
    ten green bottles, ten years in a decade,
    twice ten shillings in a pound.'

Norah:
> 'We count everything in dozens in the garden
> and in the poultry house,
> from cabbage plants to hens' eggs,
> and there are eight notes in a scale,
> seven wonders of the world,
> four cardinal points of the compass,
> three Persons in the Holy Trinity,
> nine First Fridays,
> five wise and five foolish virgins,
> six continents if you divide America in two
> leaving out the North and the South Pole,
> and six days it took to create the world,
> if you omit the seventh on which the Lord rested
> and surveyed what he had made.
> Eleven is the only odd one out between one and twelve,
> and there were eleven good disciples minus Judas.'

The monsignor:
> 'Religion and folklore
> are pervaded by seven and twelve:
> seven deadly sins, seven Labours of Hercules,
> seven Sorrows of the Blessed Virgin,
> twelve Apostles, twelve days of Christmas,
> twelve months in the year;
> but ten was the unit of the ancient world,
> the French Revolution and the Napoleonic code
> ordering Europe for perpetuity
> in metres and grammes,
> while imperial dozens ruled the roost
> from Mafeking to Mandalay.
> From that, you may deduce, if you will,
> that Fascism is, at its heart, a pragmatic code,
> while the British Empire, built on the steady virtues
> of tea and common sense,
> remains loyal to multiples of the organic twelve.'

Norah:

> 'Tuesday fortnight, exactly seventeen days away.
> I remember from the schoolroom
> that seventeen is the oddest of all the prime numbers,
> and it's all the time the pair of you have left now
> to riddle this question out.'

The Trip

The acquisitions librarian
could not have been more accommodating.
Venetia's simple catalogue was not a misstep
and the book crates would be dealt with
as they arrived, however many volumes they contained.

Having finished their business in double-quick time,
with the bishop's car purloined for the day
and plenty of rationed petrol in the tank,
the monsignor decided to take the long way home
and introduce his passenger to the Celtic Church.

It was thus that, a fortnight and three days later,
on a mild and breezy April afternoon,
Venetia and Aubrey walked through lines of ancient trees
towards the round tower at Glendalough.

The Uncertainty

She had seen many a deserted Norman keep
and walked the mounds left by ring forts
but never come anywhere near
the geometric perfection of a monastic round tower.
Almost an abstract dwelling,
its conical roof reaching to the deity in the sky,
its cylindrical base sunk into the solid, uneven ground,
its single door set so high in a wall so sheer and tight
that only Norsemen with impossible powers
could breach its hermetic cunning,
the epitome of the early Church,
a blend of piety and precision engineering
on which Aubrey held forth.

'A time when the monk, the scribe and the warrior were one,
when life and all its sciences were an integrated whole
leading to God and the service of God.
Gaelic Ireland achieved this equilibrium of talents
long before the humanist Renaissance
which invented the *uomo universale*,
equal parts soldier, scholar and politician,
this time a patrician and secular ideal
to express the possibilities of the mind,
believing it the source from which
all spiritual endeavour springs
and where it finds its fulfilment.
This formula left no place
for the eternity of the Lord.
Long ago it may seem,
but it was the beginning of the end
when Man declared himself his own religion.

Amongst the Celts there were kings and a high king,
their courts and their poets, and the Brehon Laws,
but the monks, not the nobles,
were the masters of poetry and the word,
to them, and to the brehons,
all well-born young men came to learn.
Poetry was life itself: politics, history, genealogy, topology, art,
and chiefly, in unsurpassable understatement, faith.
God and nature were at the centre of the world, interchangeable,
and this was an island of Saints and Scholars,
an oasis of calm off a battle-scarred continent,
long before those impenetrable towers were needed
to defend against Viking incursion,
before the great medieval cathedrals arose
in their mystical splendour and worldliness.'

His words made it easy for her to see
how the lucidity of purpose embodied
in such a simple stone structure
ensured its survival
when much more complicated edifices
crumbled over time.
It reached up as a symbol of purity,
like the clean, limestone steeple
of her own parish church,
piercing the sky in pursuit of the Trinity,
though the flags and plaques and pews
in memory of the wealthy and influential dead
would have impressed neither the brehons nor the monks.

'What you have grown up with
is more blended into the fabric of the state,
your bidding prayers,
the regimental insignia.
Ours is rooted in the land,
in resistance and subterfuge, on the one hand,
but in absolute belief and in the Latin Rite as well.
Apart from transubstantiation,
in which you believe as an article of faith
and we reproduce a commemorative act,
plus discrepancy on Marian devotion,
we descend in similar measure
from the community once clustered here.
Your church is a child of the arguments of its time,
more reasonable and authentic than most.

Even the most high-minded priest will admit, in private,
that religion, like politics, is a game for pragmatists
and a congregation, like an electorate,
is best moved by conviction.
Thus your Mission demagogues campaigning
from one raucous hustings to another
preaching condemnations of Anglican belief.
But faith is elusive and most of us in the priesthood
are in constant need of spiritual assurance,
to the extent that my own doubts are often a shock to myself.
That is why I find this place so comforting.
These monks had certainty,
at least, it seems they had.
Our world increasingly has none.'

The Licence

He had not expected it to come so suddenly,
nor without warning.
Those anchorite monks like St Kevin
in his cave on the Upper Lake
had not been tantalised
like he, living among women,
and yet, until her tranquil presence
burst upon his consciousness,
he had been able to state, sincerely,
in the teeth of the fleshpots of Rome
and the laxity of skull-capped prelates
that his vocation was intact.

Now, in the freedom of the forest,
licensed by proximity to a more fluid past,
when there were mixed religious establishments
and married couples within that blend,
even if the hierarchy saw fit to deny the truth,
like a baffled pagan before the smooth, stone tower,
he felt drawn by atavistic force.
'I was not ordained for this, I am honest',
he yearned to say but could not,
instead he ached with longing to assault
the citadel that was her body,
that was the mind he could not fathom,
that was the soul behind those peridot eyes,
though he knew already, dully,
there would be no response.

As she gazed at the tower,
luminous in form, opalescent of spirit,
he saw she was, as far as his travail went,
completely unaware
and thus what he meant to say
in this parlous moment
would be left, shuddering and betrayed,
a castaway on an inhospitable shore,
but still he could not stop himself.

'I sometimes think, you know,
that your church has the right of it,
that priests should be able to marry
and live fully in the world,
have a wife, have children.
Perhaps we do a disservice to ourselves
and to our flock by keeping
so much apart, a chosen elite.
The argument that the ties of the world
make us less available in times of need,
that it is too difficult to live,
a man amongst men but otherwise apart,
is not absolute,
it wasn't for the Celts.
Indeed, being father to a family
would bring us closer to what it is to be human,
to all those made of the same
flesh and blood.'

She did not react.
'Do you have any idea
of what I'm getting at',
and then he hesitated,
about to stake, as well he knew,
his whole immortal soul,
'my dear Venetia?'

The Failure

A woman attempting to seduce him
would have seen the declaration
she had schemed for.
The anguish in his voice would have told her
what his words could not
and she might, later on and in private,
have nudged herself into his devastated arms.

They might have had Elysium for a while,
if she had loved him.
Or she might have responded to his pain
with suffering of her own,
the impossibility of anything
truly existing between them,
given who they were
and from whence they came.
They might have said an exquisite farewell,
after a long and bittersweet confession
of mutual devotion and combined despair.

Both thoughts strangled his gut,
because it was all in vain.
His was seed which fell on marbled ground,
onto a self-contained, exclusive paradise.
Her back turned as she gazed at the tower,
he watched as she barely registered his plea.
After a long pause, entirely typical
but excruciating to him now,
she observed offhand, still facing the tower,
that it was rare for Protestant clergy to be unmarried,
as if they had merely been discussing
ecumenical affairs,
but when she eventually turned around,
he saw that her eyes were afire
with a different flame.
She asked him to tell her more about what went on
all those centuries ago in Glendalough.

He had lost her to the early Christian Church.
It was no comfort to him then,
nor would it be for years to come.

IV

The Scribe, 1954

The Convert

The fifties found Venetia in Rome,
capable though not fluent in Italian,
conversant with Vatican libraries and museums,
secretary to an Art History professor
and one-time model in a New York department store,
chasing down the life and work
of an overlooked female painter,
the Romantic era portraitist,
Caterina Dorotea Castelnuovo,
of whom little or nothing was known.

Venetia was now a Catholic,
instructed by a confessor
who saw in her one of that multitude who,
towards the end of the war,
turned for sanctuary to the certainties
offered in Church, Latinity and Pope.

The arrival of the first, tiny crow's feet
and a couple of undulating grey hairs
deepened her quality of enigma
and she sailed on, implacable,
though hearts foundered in her wake
with unending regularity.
The abstraction which had once cast a veil
over her youthful bloom
now become the chief fascination
of her inward maturity.

The Victory

Less than a month after Glendalough,
Aubrey left to prepare for the overseas missions,
citing a desire to get back
to the fundamentals of his faith.
In fact, his choice had been
between walking away from his vocation
or leaving the comfort he had enjoyed
the entirety of his life
to atone for the aborted betrayal
of his priestly ordination.
In the end, he chose the more arduous path
and set sail for West Africa after the bombing of Japan.

To her dying day, Josie was sure
that Venetia was at the root of it all
while the others saw in his decision
confirmation of a deeper call.
When it became known,
Venetia's conversion to the true faith
was hailed as the jewel
in his proselytiser's crown.

The Informant

Until their deaths,
the sisters kept Venetia abreast
of the monsignor's movements
and then it was Josie who could not let go.

'We laid Miss Nellie to rest today,
the Lord have mercy on her soul.
She was not long following
her dear departed sister.

Miss Nellie and Miss Norah said in the will
they would like you to have one of the miniatures.
Bishop Davouren D'Arcy says you should have
the one of the Portuguese lady,
it would be right after all the work you did in the library.

He was home, you see, from the Congo
and able to say the High Mass.
It was a pity you could not return for the funeral
but the continent is a long way away.
I am sure Miss Nellie and Miss Norah look down
from their garden in heaven and bless you.

The bishop was pleased to hear how well you have done.
He always mentioned you in his letters to the ladies.
I used to read to them when their eyesight got bad.
When I told him you were now in Rome
with Professor Madeleine Stoddart
he said "at the seat of the Church, how grand",
and "who would have thought that Miss Wallace
would end up next door to the Vatican
when she came to us a Protestant
all those years ago?"

Well, time to finish now.
I'll send you the ladies' obituary
when it comes out.'

The Gladiatrix

Carefully preserved by Germans and Allies alike,
the city looked yellow,
jaundiced by her recent intractable past,
a playground still for the monied
but barely habitable to her own dispossessed
and prey once more to acquisitive foreigners
teaching her better to exploit her photogenic cachet:
the Trevi Fountain choked with new-minted cents,
the Coliseum, a novelty carousel
for the pastel scooters of heedless expats,
the Spanish Steps overrun by dollar-rich matrons,
their sullen teenagers in tow,
clamouring for what they had been sold as authentic,
the *dolce vita* that only Rome could bestow.

Madeleine and Venetia were part of this invasion,
long-term residents with sufficient means
to rent a seven-roomed apartment with a general maid,
though Madeleine had links through marriage,
her lawyer husband, lost at the Battle of Midway,
the son of migrant labourers from the Mezzogiorno.
They met on the boat, married on arrival,
spent their long lives comfortably in Brooklyn
and named their son Ulise after the Union general, Grant
and their own sea voyage to a better life.

Those simple, loving peasants would have been agog
at the sheer magnificence of their late son's erstwhile wife,
as that afternoon Professor Stoddart set out
on the trail of a Catarina Dorotea find,
an Afghan hound, silken and stealthy,
in mother-of-pearl suit and dove-coloured gloves,
blonde chignon and beige pillbox hat.
No more than a decade older than Venetia,
time had made her fine-boned features aquiline
and, whether for work or pleasure,
she bestrode the Roman streets like a gladiatrix,
eye-catching, dominant, in command,
even as the contrast with Venetia's diaphanous naiad
rendered them a traffic-stopping pair
in that melancholy hour of tarnished grandeur
with New World largesse once again required
to paste a veneer over mouldering despair.

The Sermon

Amadeo Trentini, parish priest of Civitavecchia, c.1805

The soul of the female is an inherently unclean thing,
likewise what we may call the imagination,
although to compare this faculty in the female
to that of her God-ordained natural superior, the male,
would be as to liken the sparrow to the eagle in the sky,
an abomination.

The mind of the female is polluted,
as is her body, open she to all manner of pestilence
without means of discerning its evil aforethought.

A female is not made for creation in herself,
merely gestation as the vessel of the male,
immediately following upon which it has been ordained
that her body and the infant be cleansed of her stain
through holy writ and ritual before re-admittance
to the Blessed Sacraments may be entertained.

Yet, who will stand in vigilance
over the incubi of her unstable mind,
who will protect unsuspecting humanity
from the infested void
that is the brain of a woman?

The Apostate

Venetia:
    'This Fr Trentini was certainly extreme.
    Sometimes the mission priests came close,
    on the subjects of drink, indolence
    and, inevitably, Protestants,
    but I suppose he lived
    a long time ago now.'

Madeleine:
    'But it's not for priests to decide, is it,
    whatever they may think themselves?
    Oh, don't be so shocked, you know very well
    what I think of the institution
    of the Catholic Church.
    Private devotion such as yours
    is quite a different thing.
    It's the public face
    I have such difficulty with.

    "The apostate Professor Stoddart,
    Maddy Stoddart who doesn't even use
    her late husband's name any more".

Why did I do that? I haven't told you, have I?
Because he cheated on me.
If he hadn't been killed in the war
we would have been divorced anyway.
"The divorced, apostate Professor Stoddart".
Hell, I'll even go one better.
A year after we married
when he was just finishing Law School
I had an abortion,
I couldn't afford to give up work
because he had to finish his degree
if we were ever going to make anything of ourselves.

"The might-have-been divorced,
apostate, aborted-in-a-dump Professor Stoddart,
who doesn't even use her war hero husband's name!"

What would this ultramontane Trentini have said
if he came across me?
A university woman, an apostate
and a murderer of unborn children.
Am I not the very pestilence he preached against?'

Venetia:
    'In the Blitz I was courted by a man
    who was blown up by a bomb
    in a tree behind a park bench.
    He died. I was there too
    and spent eighteen months
    a convalescent.
    It was the will of God.'

The Reaction

Madeleine was speechless, appalled at herself,
to have touched real pain with a cynical, showy gambit,
a lowdown trick worthy of her lowest, most bootlegging days.
Suddenly, it was more than she could bear.
Worse, she had used the abortion as a ploy,
that awfulness which, ever since it had taken place,
had been unspeakable, except in paroxysm.

In dreams she saw, with cruel, unrelenting regularity,
the happy-go-lucky, man-in-the-moon face
of that downy child who would be an adult by now,
watched as it was pierced and dismembered
by a long, slicing needle, then thrown in a bin,
abandoned in a vacuum that was eternally hers.

Venetia's wounds,
though she had no right to disturb them,
would have been a blessing in comparison,
her composure showing there were no regrets,
only cool resignation,
so she pulled herself back, this time from real passion,
to mark her respect.

'You are very lucky, Venetia,
that you can accept
the will of God.
On me, it has no such effect.'

The Homage

On a street across the river from Castel Sant' Angelo,
a museum since the early twentieth century,
once home of the proud and indomitable Orsini,
once Hadrian's family mausoleum,
in Caterina Dorotea's time, a gaol
in which she was incarcerated for a week,
two old friends sat at their usual café,
as tourists nearby frequented another of the sites
their guidebooks labelled 'must see'.

A life-long socialist and scholar through and through,
Manlio chose exile rather than recantation
and so while *il Duce* prospered,
he taught beefy mid-Western boys
more taken by his resemblance
to a woebegone Fred Astaire
than anything Italian literature had to offer.
Prairie campus life discomfited him
but it was nothing to what he had to bear
when the United States entered the war
and, despite his record of principled dissent,
Professor Giovanelli was interned as an alien suspect.

Without Madeleine and many others
he would not have survived
with either his career or his mind intact.
In his later detention camp letters,
he encouraged her to study,
arguing that scholarship,
his solace through the years of exile,
would alleviate her grief and consternation
and he was proven correct.
These days they were colleagues
and equals as of right.

He was engaged in the delicate business
of exonerating the life and achievements
of the fourteenth-century Roman Tribune,
the inn-keeper's son Cola di Rienzo,
whose end had not been unlike that of Mussolini.
It had been a predictably obdurate enterprise
in that post-war, Marshall Plan milieu
but that Summer, the exchange of views
between Madeleine and Manlio began to gravitate
in a rather different direction.

'Madeleine, it is the anniversary of Cola's return to Rome,
the first of August, six hundred years ago, today.
From now, it will be a day short of ten weeks to his death,
his betrayal by his love of rings and bracelets.'

A man whose wits had grown as bloated as his belly,
only forty years old but a mere chimera
of the demagogue who aspired to be the equal of Christ.
No gardener, unless he were a thief,
would have owned such precious things
and in their anger, the people knew it,
tearing him and his disguise apart,
their vengeance remorseless,
as it was with Mussolini
when he showed himself to be
not a Messiah but an empty vessel of a man.

'This is one of the sad truths of my people,
we are always taken in by these men of straw.
I know you have listened to this before,
but today it is a question of homage
and you will understand.'

She nodded, somewhat puzzled.

'Now, of course, you and I, my dear,
must be the only people choosing to pass
this terrible month here, but for good reasons,
you for Caterina Dorotea, I, because I feel that,
for one last time, I must relive his steps.'

'What do you mean, one last time?'

'I think I will go away when it is over.
The book is almost finished,
there will be no more reason to remain.'

'You mean you will leave Rome?'

'I've been a wanderer for a long time.
Do not worry. Something will turn up.
I will know where when the time comes.'

The *Vie de Bohème*

'Why nothing more nor less, my dear,
than to throw everything up, just like that,
on the ninth of October, which is the day after
the six hundredth anniversary of Cola's death.
And he tells me he has no plans.
He's going to leave Rome
but he won't say where he's going,
he says he doesn't know.
He won't have a job,
he'll live on his savings.
Can you imagine?
The true *vie de bohème*.

Oh, Rome is such a splendid, eternal city,
you feel that all things are possible here,
that dreams do come true.
Mamma Roma will look benignly on his venture,
I know she will.
Don't you ever feel the same urge yourself,
to cast caution once and for all to the winds
and see what life will throw up for you?
Why should we be tied to this workaday life?'

'Monsignor Davouren D'Arcy went
off to the missions in the Congo very suddenly.
By all accounts he has been very happy there.'

'The Congo, darling, that reminds me
– *Mogambo*, have you seen it?
You must, even if the story is a bit perverse,
the soundtrack is genuine tribal,
it would give you a sense
of what assails the missionaries' ears.
He went off suddenly, did you say?'

'He'd been at the Vatican before that,
then came home to be diocesan secretary.'

'That's unusual for the Church.
Did anyone know why?
Anywhere I've been, an event like that
would have kept the tongues wagging for months.
For a Curia-trained monsignor to drop everything
and go the Congo on a whim,
why it's preposterous.
But, perhaps not, perhaps not.'

Venetia agreed and Madeleine continued.

'You're right, after all, it's what Manlio is doing.
I don't know why he's made that decision
and I know him better than anybody in Rome.
How well did you know the monsignor, Venetia?
Heavens, you're not the reason he left, are you?
I wonder if there's someone like that in Manlio's case,
some woman he hasn't mentioned.
You never know, the world is full of men
who never mention other women,
my late unlamented husband for one,
oh dear, what a ramble.
Will you forgive me, honey?
I think I'll go and lie down.
Today has been just that bit too much.'

The Dancers

In Rome, she did not have a sense
of intimacy with nature,
not like Shrathancrur or Glendalough,
only the geraniums on the terrace
came close to seeming immanence
and then in a rather whimsical fashion:
the pinkish ones translucent
whatever the angle of the sun,
the darker flowers more solid,
creatures of the street-lit night.
She named them for the dancing beaux
who would waft through fluted colonnades
and gardenia-scented nights,
the St Johns, Maximillians and Sergeys
of black-and-white Art Deco balls
on the antebellum Riviera
in all its languid excess,
before the war altered everything,
admittedly for the better.

'Venetia, my dear, what in heaven's name
has put that smile on your face?
Is there something going on
that I should know about?'

'You mean the geraniums?'

'The geraniums?'

'I was thinking about their names.'

'You mean the genus and all that?'

'No, pet names.'

'For Pete's sake, why?'

'They look like dancers.
The men are the stems
and the flowers are the women in their arms.
They remind me of balls when I was young:
Agatha and Sergey on the left,
Violet and Maximillian in the middle,
Cicely and St John on the right.
I mean the society photos in magazines.
The men were always down from Oxford,
back from India or off to Cowes
and all living it up in the South of France.'

Madeleine turned sardonic.

'And looking like Fred Astaire, I suppose,
just like Manlio Giovanelli
though I can't see him indulging
in that sort of fare.
You're right, they do look like figurines,
Lalique with a cosier edge, you might say.
I spent most of the twenties modelling dresses
for women who could have been at all those balls.
The season, how antiquated now!
One of them was even presented at court,
although nobody could figure out why
when she was Texas bred and New York born.

But you know your three geranium couples
remind me of something much more up-to-date?
My dear Venetia, they could be *Three Coins in the Fountain*,
that new film about American secretaries over here?
There was a trailer for it when we went to see *Roman Holiday*.
Three girls meet three very different men
and all live happily ever after at the end.
The song says so anyway.
We must try to see it when it comes out,
then you can tell me if your geranium ballerinas approve.
We can make it part of a new campaign
to enjoy ourselves more,
take a bit of time off from Caterina Dorotea
and the labyrinthine, dusty vaults.'

The Affair

August wore on.
Caterina Dorotea caused a scandal
when one of the archives threw up,
as its final offering, a daybook-cum-diary
in which she chronicled an affair
with the poet André Chénier,
an acquaintance formed at a fashionable salon
during the brief trip he made to Italy
before the Revolution.
There was a series of hinted-at trysts,
correspondence from him in French and Italian
truncated when he was arrested by mistake.
She was then a respectable married woman
and a mother of three.
The common belief had been
that, apart from her children,
she had lived only for her art.
Madeleine was incandescent.

'Manlio *mio*, Can you believe it?
Thirty-one years of age,
cut off in the prime of his life,
only three days before the end of the Terror?
Is there a God in heaven to allow such a thing?
And she was so happy,
you can tell from her entries on his letters,
truly happy for possibly the only time in her life.
That miserable husband of hers,
a sterling non-entity
in his counting house like some Gradgrind,
or better still Mr Casaubon!
Imagine if George Eliot had sent Will Ladislaw
off to the Crimean War soldiering,
never to be seen again?
Oh, life is so unfair, it is so wrong
for her to have found all that and then
to have lost it so very, very soon.
Three more days to the execution of Robespierre
and he would have been safe to grow old with her.
Oh, I know what you're going to say,
we don't know what she actually wrote to Chénier
and Caterina Dorotea would not have left her husband,
but I remind you that he died three years later.

Three days to live and three years to happiness
but they couldn't have it.'

The Prison

Manlio:

'It sounds as if they had perfection for a short time.
Is that not more than most of us may ever aspire to?'

Madeleine:

'But don't you think some people are gifted with perfection
and don't have to strive for it as much as others?'

Manlio:

'Mortals like ourselves?'

Madeleine:

'Look at Caterina Dorotea and Chénier.
They enjoyed the full expression of their art
when they were hardly out of their teens.
They never had to go in search of it like the rest of us.
Think of the *Contadine at Dusk*.'

Manlio:

'Painted when she was only sixteen?'

Madeleine:

'The first sketches at sixteen, yes,
a couple of framed pastels,
cartoons for tapestries, a bit like Goya.
You know the kind of thing,
rosy-cheeked maidens and curly-haired youths
dancing around bunches of grapes and carafes of Chianti
with a nondescript city in the distance.
The final version, in oils, came several years later,
the first time the city backdrop is recognisably Rome,
with Castel' Sant Angelo in a prominent position
and the whole is much darker in tone.

No more carefree young bloods and wenches,
just women and girls this time, with individual faces,
and tangible anguish in the lines round their eyes.'

Manlio:
'Castel Sant' Angelo was a Papal fortress in Cola's time,
but up to the French invasion
a dungeon for political detainees.'

Madeleine:
'And she was held there briefly herself,
but now she's being very precise:
Castel Sant' Angelo stands for the *Grand Terreur*.
Long before the French marched into Rome,
she's pointing to those prisons that succeeded the Bastille.'

Manlio:
'The Luxembourg Palace.
At least that's where Danton
and Desmoulins were held.
I would be surprised if Chénier
were not confined in the same place.'

Madeleine:
'And in the painting there's a woman with her back turned,
looking up into the battlements of the *castello*.
You can't see her face and you can't see what she's looking at,
I always thought she must be some obscure allegorical character
but it's Caterina Dorotea herself, looking up in despair.'

Manlio:
     'Sometimes, death is easier, at least there's a clean break.'

Madeleine:
     'Which brings us to my mysterious Venetia.
     She had an excellent recommendation
     from my cousin in Dublin but all he said
     was that she worked for an old Catholic family
     on a private collection dating from eighteen six or seven.
     Now she's begun to mention a monsignor she was close to,
     Rome-trained, who went to the Congo all of a sudden.
     Before that there was a fiancé
     blown to bits by a bomb in London
     and she nearly accompanied him to Kingdom Come.
     She seems so utterly accepting.
     I can hardly understand it.
     Perhaps it's time the two of you met.'

The Introduction

Their flat, off the Campo de' Fiori,
had views of the *castello* and Capitol Hill,
this latter, with the adjacent Piazza Campidoglio,
being the site of Cola di Rienzo's last stand.

'Poor Cola's doom on one side
and Caterina Dorotea's on the other, Madeleine?'

'Don't be so morose.
You'll give Venetia the wrong impression
when she comes back from the store.
Now I see why we've always met in cafés.
How can I possibly introduce you to my friends
when you are such a comedian?'

'Irony, so rare in your race.'

'I often wish it weren't so plentiful in yours.'

When he and Venetia were introduced,
Manlio beheld his own Capuchin state,
the contemplative's eye on another world,
godless in his case, reflected in her face.
Spiritualità francescana, he mused.
Whether she knew about it or not,
he thought he understood.

The Conversation

On the terrace,
the talk turned to antiquity.
Manlio spoke of Cola's love of pageantry
and his seven-month attempt
to re-establish Ancient Rome.
'As all dictators do, he began all over again,
tabula rasa in thirteen forty-seven,
Year One of the Restoration of the Roman Republic.'

Madeleine was about to advise Venetia
to watch out for herself,
take out a good insurance policy.
She had observed that one never knew
what might happen when new people
like Cola or Robespierre arose,
and, unlike herself and Manlio
who had brought it upon themselves,
she was an innocent passing through
and should have safe passage prepared just in case.

Venetia was off, however,
but on a different track.
'Does this put Christianity
on a par with dictatorship?'
She went on.
'The birth of Christ is a zero too
and everywhere the Gospel spread
the monks imposed their calendar.
When they went to Ireland
no-one there would have known
they were in the year four thirty-two.
Their time went back to Cúchulainn,
Maeve and Fionn MacCumhaill,

the legends of Gaelic antiquity.
No-one knows how far back they go.'

Manlio interjected.
'Nonetheless, Ireland accepted the new faith
with alacrity, is that not true?'

She seemed not to have heard.
'It was the Island of Saints and Scholars.
When the Vikings came
the monks built high towers
and stored their manuscripts and treasures
up in the air away from the longboats,
with doors fifteen feet off the ground.
The pirates couldn't use fire as a weapon
because the round towers
were completely made of stone.
The monks must have felt very close to God,
and they made beautiful books.'

Manlio tried again.
'Like the Book of Kells?
I wish I had seen it.'

This time he had tuned to the right frequency.
'On one there was a little poem,
about a monk and his white cat,
called *Pangur Bán*.
The cat caught mice in his claws,
the monk unravelled problems in his mind
and they were both happy in their work.
The world to them was an afterthought,
and so were its desires.'

Upon which Manlio knew his initial impression
had been sumptuously right.
'Have you ever been attracted
by the religious life, Signorina Venetia?'

She responded, directly this time.
'Monsignor Davouren D'Arcy went to the missions.
It was after he showed me Glendalough.
If I had been a nun back then
perhaps I would have gone along.'

He pursued his point.
'The Good Lord says it's never too late
to change your life if you must.'

She continued.
'I almost married during the war.
There were endless bombs
and people in burning houses to evacuate.
It was no different to cats stuck on eaves,
most could have found their own way down as well.
If we had been like the monks,
there would have been no war.'

Then he attempted to lighten the mood,
he knew Madeleine was about to explode.
'You mean we would have been safe
if we were monks sitting cross-legged and serene
on the branch of a tall, friendly tree?'

But she made another sideways move.
'In London the bomb was in a tree.
It was a sad way for a journalist's life to end.
They're not supposed to become the story.'

At which, though forewarned,
he could only come up with a platitude.
'Unfortunately, we are all only too mortal.'

She carried on.
'The monks in the round tower
knew nothing of war,
only how to avoid it.
It seemed the correct way to me.
Rome, all the same, is different.
Pope Gregory the Great saw an angel
sheathing a sword on the Castel Sant'Angelo
when there was a great plague
and we are now in the centenary year
of *Ineffabilis Deus*, the longed-for doctrine
of the Immaculate Conception.'

She had not lost him yet.
'You mean the Church is still vibrant and holy?
I'm not so sure, Signorina.
Much that has happened would have embittered
anyone but your tranquil monks.'

Madeline wanted to say that the New Look
did more for morale than Catholicism ever could,
to fulminate about the nepotism, hypocrisy,
the antediluvian conservatism of the Vatican
and Pius XII's inability to stand up to the fascists,
but she was disconcerted by the instant rapport
between her old friend and her new companion.
Theirs was a ruminative kind of complicity
in which for her there was neither hand, act nor part,
though there was no erotic charge in question,
of that she was one hundred per cent certain.

The Concert

The auditorium was filled
with high-spending tourists,
gaudy colours and twanging vowels
overrunning the old country
as if it was a Disneyland attraction
bought and paid for
in trauma and dollar bills
when they entered the war
and mortgaged it to the hilt.

The Cola-Caterina trio
were of the other school,
attentive to the orchestra,
reading the programme notes,
grateful for what was owed
but secure in what was theirs to own,
Venetia, that evening, more than most.

She was always puzzled that people expected her
to respond to an idea or gambit
as if she could grab it out of the air like a javelin
while it was still on its outbound flight
and send it spinning back towards them
before she had any idea of where it would land
or how the perforated earth might react,
when the only possible reply could be
whatever the ruptured ground chose to emit.

In snatches over the course of that evening,
she conveyed this and some of the following
to an attentive Manlio as they stayed in their seats
while their gregarious companion
went off to mingle with some people she had met.

When I went home after the bomb
everyone thought I had been engaged,
some people even thought he was very wealthy.
Those were the ideas coming out of their minds,
I could not get inside to challenge them.

I used to be called Vinnie Fixit,
but there was nothing unusual in what I did.
Those people in the Blitz
had all been brought up in the city.
They could only see the streets
as bricks and mortar,
everything created to restrict.
I saw them as furze bushes on a marshy hill.
If your boot gets stuck in a bog,
you twist it and out it comes,
pull and you will be forever stuck.
If a furze bush gets in your way,
you bend it and pass by,
it will bounce back.
If you find yourself
at the bottom of a spongy hill,
go up zig-zag and sideways,
you will not feel the incline that way
and you will not slip.
Those city people did not know
that landscape is what you make it,
they only knew about possessions.

George thought it was natural
to own things and people,
within reason,
but I had nothing to give,
how could I when there is nothing living
that can be held in the hand?

Seánie Milligan lived
beside a place of magical trees,
he talked to horses and they understood him,
he did not try to put a fence around them
but he was trapped in the end
and I had to leave.

Only the monks were truly free.
That is why I converted,
to follow their way, to be inside my soul.
The monsignor went to the Congo,
I expect for the same reason.

I was tied to dreams
of gallant young men once.
I named the geraniums for some.
Now they are gone.
You are told when you are young
that there are rose-scented rooms
and dashing beaux
to sweep you off your feet
but this is not life
and it is why I am now a scribe.

The *Flâneurs*

Manlio decided to let August be,
in all its heat and oppression,
satisfied now that he had made his decision.

The three spent a lot of time touring together,
unbuttoned in holiday *déshabille*.
'You can take the fashion from the girl
but you cannot take the girl from fashion',
was Madeleine's parting cry as she abandoned them,
bare-headed, *sans* parasol, for some inland couturier.
There was no point taking Venetia along,
she was not predatory about her attire.
She had a small array of Victorian jewellery
and she was partial to gold-threaded shawls.
These lent her an air of Nordic mystery
which never failed to strike the Roman *flâneurs*,
though she appeared impervious to them,
even when they performed the adolescent ritual
of pinching her behind when she walked alone.
Manlio, who had aped his elders as a child
and would forever feel suitably begrimed,
grinned to see these cut-price Lotharios
embarrassed, crestfallen, undermined,
and yearned for a less distracted voluptuary
to turn on them her righteous ire,
though not Madeleine of course,
or there would be murder charges and lawyers to hire.

In September, he gave his manuscript to his publisher
with a dedication to his dearest friends,
dottoressa Madeleine Stoddart
and the late Theodore Ulysses Zingaretti.
After the loss of his wife and stillborn twins,
Ulise had taken him, heartsore and faltering, under his wing,
then Madeleine, once widowed, became his close friend.
His long-lost Lucia had been his childhood sweetheart,
he had never afterwards considered anyone else,
thus it was Madeleine above all his friends
on whom he depended to understand
and facilitate what he had planned.

But Madeleine had begun to keep her distance.
Her boutique sprees were partly a means
of allowing the other two time on their own,
partly a vent for her utter bewilderment
at feeling suddenly bereft and alone.
Frustration drove her to throw them together
as often and as much as she could,
so that whatever it was would declare itself.
Venetia simply observed, once in a while,
that Madeleine was more frantic than was her wont
but Manlio knew she had divined
that something more than mere restlessness was afoot.

The Rationale

It was nearing the end of September
when Manlio asked to see Madeleine on her own
at their usual spot on the Via Paola.
The weather had cooled
and the city had taken back its Summer egress
of mothers and school-age children from the hills,
with the patriarchs who had spent
at least a couple of weeks on the family beaches,
and then a couple more in the city
in the arms of a much younger *maîtresse*.

Madeleine felt leaden bells pounding in her heart
when he asked to meet at this rendezvous.
She was sure he was about to declare
some sort of commitment to Venetia.
Though she knew such a thing
was completely improbable,
the damage to their easy fellowship
would be nigh on unbearable.

'I've almost forgotten who Caterina Dorotea is,
there have been so many lovely hats and dresses of late.'

'It will take a long time for those boutiques
to recover from your whirlwind visits.
Did you buy anything at all?'

'Not a scrap. Inferior quality. No flair.'

Her dismissal had nothing to do
with that Summer's fashions.
It was uncomfortable
and he was trying to be jocose.
They lapsed into the first awkward silence
of their decades-long companionship.
He stirred his coffee in its tiny cup
and she averted her gaze
to stare without seeing
at the battlements
of the Castel Sant' Angelo.

Then she tried, in her turn,
ashamed of the cowardice
to which she had given in.
'The *castello* looks rather fierce
and satisfied with itself today,
don't you think?
This was all he needed to begin.

'A venerable old place with a belligerent history.
Cola should have taken refuge there on his last day,
instead of trusting in his games of disguise.
He should have put his faith,
however compromised by the venal world, in God,
the whole point of the Middle Ages, faith over reason.
He used pageantry full of mythological emblems
and mystical symbols in his pomp, theatre as ritual,
and when the time came to gamble for his life,
he tried a mask of normality
but forgot the golden rings and bracelets he still wore.
The mob beat him to death,
dragged him along the Corso
and hung his corpse by the heels
for two days outside the church of San Marcello.
They did that, Madeleine,

because what they found was not their tribune,
bedecked in all the hermetics of medieval heraldry,
the one who had created himself their saviour;
nor the plain man of the people,
the senator in the old Roman style
he might and should have been.
They found a monster on the street,
a peasant with jewelled fingers and wrists
who could not see the incongruity of his dress.
If he had known himself for what he was,
a Medieval demagogue,
and left the ancient city, the Coliseum and the Forum
to come over to the Castel Sant' Angelo on the Vatican side,
he might have survived.
That he did not is why he died.'

He continued.
'To get to this, I asked three questions of myself.
First I wanted to understand why he failed
and twice in seven years, simple history;
and how did he prefigure our recent tragicomedy,
the past illuminating the present, Mussolini.
The people once again performed the identification,
hanging *il Duce* in the same way as *il Tribuno*
and he, by trying to escape in a similar manner.
The German petty officer in the back of a truck
on its way to the Swiss border
was nothing if not a reincarnation
of Cola's aged gardener with a mattress on his back.
He wore no tell-tale rings.
He boasted to a comrade years before
that he would never be caught like Cola
because he wore no jewels.
But twenty years of omnipresence,
his face papered onto every street corner,
imprinted on him the trappings of power

as indelibly as they had been grafted onto Cola.
In costume, he was merely another *buffo*,
there to be ridiculed.

My second question.
Why did we enter the nightmare twice?
Ancient Rome was long dead,
yet we permitted another foolish attempt
to recover a splendour and discipline
that had nothing to do with our modern polity.
Only sixty years a nation
and we allowed ourselves to be overtaken
by risible delusion.
This I could not answer.
We are still too close to the phenomenon,
and I lived too much of that time
at a distance in the American Mid-West.

The only question I could put to myself,
and the only one I could reasonably answer,
relates to my own culpability
and what my actions should be now?'

'But you did everything you could,
they were about to throw you and Lucia in gaol.
You lost everything,
you said everything that could be said.
You ask too much of yourself.'

This was the frankness she had loved so much,
these were the preoccupations she knew
for as long as she had counted him her dearest friend.
Now, after her long month of doubt and alienation,
she felt restored, witness to the charting
of the next instalment of his life,
first mate in charge of navigation.

The Invitation

'Venetia has made of herself a vestal
so she can remain hermetically sealed
like the monks in the tower
and she wants nothing more.
My truth is more involved.
I have lived very much in the world,
travelled, written, thought, loved
then lost those I cared for,
except you Madeleine.
What I have to tell you now
will neither be easy nor quick
but bear with me to the end.

I have made no contribution to national life.
I left when I should have stayed,
allowed myself to become a very minor patriot.
I have come to believe that it was an act of cowardice,
unwitting then, but to be condemned nonetheless.
I chose to interrogate Cola because Mussolini was too close
and because it was vital to arrive at a re-evaluation.
Cola's was the type of vainglorious tyranny
that drove thousands into exile in our century,
it became my responsibility to try to find some good in it
so the two reigns of Cola and the twenty-one years of Mussolini
might not be so utterly empty of value
for my countrymen and for me.
Who better to rescue the reputation of a monster
than his implacable enemy?
Who should take on the burden more than one who ran away?
For a long time, I could not see past the fascination of Cola
and I believed my labours to be of great academic worth.
Now I don't know if what I have written will have any importance.
Those who have lived into this new era, understandably,
just want to move on.

So I came back to my own responsibility in this
and I saw that there was only one step remaining:
a more particular sacrifice of myself.
Though I knew this by intuition,
I could not understand why, beyond self-pity,
which is no honourable justification,
until I met Venetia, your second gift to me,
after your friendship.
She made me realise
that the only expectation laid on us
is that we find then hold fast to our own truth.

They should have held their ground.
Cola should have gone to the Castel Sant' Angelo.
That he drew down on himself a grisly pantomime
was his failure, as it was Mussolini's.
I intend to enact the end they should have had.
It will be the gesture I should have made thirty years ago,
a debt discharged late, but paid all the same.'

'Are you ill, Manlio?
I don't mean to take from what you've just said,
but it would help me to know.'

'I'm in perfect health, for my age,
But I am ready to die now
and I claim the privilege
of choosing the time, the place and the manner,
as the old Romans used to.
Please make no attempt to gainsay me.
In the end it will happen anyway,
an act that will finally undo my cowardice
and through me, to an infinitesimal degree,
since I on my own am wholly inadequate,
purge the final flights of Cola and Mussolini.'

On the morning of the eighth of October,
the six-hundredth anniversary of Cola's demise,
he would be on the roof of the Castel Sant' Angelo.
He would like Madeleine and Venetia there
to watch over him and bid him adieu.

Beforehand, Venetia was not to know.
Crushed as she was by what he had just conveyed
though trying her utmost to conceal it,
his exclusion of Venetia from foreknowledge
gave her some small consolation
and she agreed to facilitate his plan.

The Pantheon

No work was to be done until the eighth.
Venetia went to Monte Cassino
as soon as travel could be arranged.

'A Benedictine monastery,
founded only a hundred years
after Christianity reached Ireland,
but no match for modern combat.
The soldiers fought without regard
for what they were trampling over.
As if Vikings had fought Normans
over the ruins of Glendalough,
there was no immunity for sacred places
from the wrath of war.'

Madeleine made stilted remarks
about the difficulty of the journey,
the morbid nature of the spectacle.

'I went to see Coventry Cathedral in England
before and then after the devastation.
There was no vendetta against God,
the building was just a casualty.
At Monte Cassino, they went over the same ground
advancing, retreating, advancing again,
so many deaths on that holy site,
so many unburied beneath those stones.'

Madeleine comprehended some of this,
though only enough to be somewhat flummoxed.
Manlio explained as best he could.

'Ah, yes, she will have to walk the earth,
see what spears will be cast into her inner landscape.
She told me this some time ago,
you were present but by then you weren't listening.
Some part of you already knew what I had in mind to do.
Then she will wait, without knowing she is waiting,
perhaps moments, perhaps days,
for what will come to her in reply.
And then this nation, Italy, too,
through the pain in the stones at Monte Cassino
will become part of her pantheon of purity,
along with the round tower of Glendalough
she speaks of so much
and the ruins of the cathedral in Coventry.'

The fey twilight of Shrathancrur
was not something she had spoken about,
but that was where her odyssey had begun,
when Seánie's tales not those of Grace had won.

The Contemplation

On the last day before the eighth, Venetia came back from Monte Cassino having spent the best part of a week in contemplation of the ruins not already undergoing reconstruction. She met Madeleine and Manlio at their Via Paola café and he invited her to watch the sun rise over the city with them the following morning, the six-hundredth anniversary of Cola's death. Then he asked her how she found the devastated monastery. This is what she thought and, in some form, may have told him:

> Benedictines pray seven times daily.
> According to their Rule,
> to be happy they must wish to be where they are,
> not elsewhere.
> All this was in the stones,
> a simple concentration on the act of being there.
>
> There is no avoiding knowledge of the shells
> and the deaths,
> but what remains is the message in the earth.
>
> I felt the same years ago in Coventry,
> the ethereality of all the hymns
> absorbed into the burnt rafters.
> Generation after generation
> of worship remained
> while the accident of bombing
> evaporated in the air.
>
> Perhaps only good intention
> survives in the end.

The Plan

'I will be on the battlements at seven thirty.
The light will be good,
the pale gold of the early sun.
I will have taken a lethal overdose.
It will not be distressing for you to watch.
When I am gone you must call an ambulance
and tell the police you arrived too late.
I want you to have my remains cremated,
then scatter the ashes on the Tiber.
Try to see if you can do it from the bridge.
In this envelope you will find
all the information you need.'

Madeleine put it away,
ready for when the time came.

'If Lucia and I had had surviving children,
if she had not died,
I would have felt obliged to stay,
though other people
are a very tenuous reason for continuing to live
after you know that your purpose has reached its end.
It is the nature of our friendship
that gives me the freedom to go as I choose.
I know it costs you greatly not to forestall me.'

The Goodbye

W.B. Yeats, 'He Wishes for the Cloths of Heaven'

At seven thirty the following morning,
not a moment sooner,
Madeleine and Venetia came out
onto the battlements
of the Castel Sant' Angelo.

Madeleine wore a dove-grey, full-skirted taffeta dress,
a silver mink stole, long grey gloves
and a five-string bracelet of dewdrop pearls.
All this she had donned for sorrow,
in spite of Manlio's instruction to the contrary.
She crowned the outfit with a lacquered coolie hat,
deep vermilion overlaid with metallic filigree.
It glinted silver in the early light,
the currency of betrayal on blood,
though what the treachery was she knew not.

Venetia came behind in a pale turquoise sheath
which fell from her shoulders in Dorian pleats
and over her arm a fine damasked shawl,
aquamarine patterned in cream and fawn.

Manlio, in a neat black suit,
was seated on a deckchair facing the Tiber,
he seemed drowsy but not quite asleep.
Wordlessly, Madeleine moved forward
and kissed him on either cheek.
'Farewell, my dear.'
She saw he had already gone,
a final act of compassion
that did not take her by surprise.
Then she took the envelope pinned to his lapel,
and read his final words.

'As my soul departs,
if indeed I have one,
I wish Venetia to read these lines
and you to hold my cooling hand.
I have loved you profoundly,
my most cherished friend,
and for these final rites
you have my eternal thanks.

Venetia came closer when Madeleine beckoned her.
'Manlio is dead, Venetia.
I have known about this for some time.
He wants you read aloud for him now.'

Without demur, Venetia intoned:

> *Had I the heavens' embroidered cloths,*
> *Enwrought with golden and silver light,*
> *The blue and the dim and the dark cloths*
> *Of night and light and the half light ...*

The Blessing

Madeleine lay coiled at his feet,
a fading swan, frozen in grief.
Venetia went up to his remains,
rolled the poem into a scroll
and placed it in his limp palms.
Then, turning her face to the nascent sun,
she stepped between them and the light
and, both arms wide above her head,
a corner of the damasked shawl in either hand,
she floated it, a princely canopy,
over the inanimate pas-de-deux beneath.

After a while,
Madeleine registered the sound
of the shawl snapping in the breeze
and looked up.
For one split second,
she thought she saw
the sword-wielding angel,
then understood it was Venetia
and came to.

'That is kind of you, honey,
but he no longer fears the heat of the sun
and you see, for once, I came equipped
with a rice-farmer's hat.'

She sighed.

'Now, I must organise
a different kind of immolation,
as was his request.'

Venetia stood guard beside Manlio's corpse,
her shawl now draped over one shoulder,
a folded wing.

> *His soul is gone up.*
> *I felt it come loose and put up my shawl*
> *so it would not fall back again.*
> *He is gone to meet Pangur Bán and his monk*
> *in that place where there is only undivided spirit,*
> *where he would have no call to be in any other,*
> *where all the stones are like those of Monte Cassino.*

The Interregnum

A year of bureaucracy and mourning ensued,
a year in which Madeleine completed the work
on her vindication of Caterina Dorotea.
It kept her somewhat distracted in those long months,
through all the milestones marking his absence,
on the journey through that year of loss.

It took time to have his body released,
complications ensued from his entanglement
with the Fascist-era police,
and there was an investigation
before the suicide could be certified.
When eventually his will was formally read
there was difficulty regarding his cremation,
then his refusal to have a Catholic interment,
a last straw for his executrix,
but he had foreseen the problems
and made provision for how they might be overcome.

He asked for Venetia to recite the Yeats poem again,
on the anniversary of his death,
as Madeleine dispersed his ashes.
At the height of her boutique-raiding rage,
she would have been incensed
that her dear friend preferred the sound
of Venetia's voice to her own,
but now, with a full year's hindsight,
it was something she could more than comprehend.

She had no idea where the soul would go after death
or indeed if there was any existence beyond the grave.
She had no innocent dreams of joining Manlio
or recovering any other idealised memory
from what had been a not very satisfactory life
when her own time of reckoning came.

In the meantime, Venetia, reserved and knowing,
made plans to go down a much different path
but held off for the moment from any avowal
in deference to Madeleine's distress.

The Dispersal

Madeleine took her place
at the parapet of the *Pons Aelius*,
the bridge of Sant'Angelo,
his ashes in a box in her silver string bag.
The task was nearly complete.
There was no permission to ask
but still they came at dawn
in order not to have to justify themselves
to a passing policeman or priest.

They wore the clothes they had worn a year before.
The light promised to be golden again
and his ashes would fall like a pewter cloud
onto the waters of the placid river below.
Venetia would recite the Yeats poem once more
as Madeleine released the remains,
her companion the necessary go-between,
between this Earth and the other world.

The rays of the sun made no inroads
on the chill of the morning,
nor did they illuminate the ash as it fell.
It could not have been more prosaic.
As she stood at the ledge,
the empty casket in her hands,
Madeleine knew her betrayal
of Manlio's tacit request
would now come to pass,
for the accumulated pain
had grown too great.
She had fulfilled, at some cost,
all his other requirements
and Venetia, she knew,

would assure their legacies
on Cola and Caterina.
So she slid onto the parapet
just as Venetia finished her recitation.

'Give me your hand, honey.'
Venetia had leaned over the edge
to watch the ashes spreading,
she did not realise what was happening
until it was too late
'Goodbye, my dear.
Be joyful for the rest of your life.
Haven't we had a ball!'

With that, Madeleine turned away
and launched herself onto the river beneath.
She fell feet first into the stately flow,
her taffeta skirt winding back over her,
a shroud to take her into the deep.
Only the quicksilver vermilion hat
remained on the surface,
in the centre of Manlio's ash.

Venetia took hold of her folded shawl,
a mortal angel on the parapet wall,
and spread it out in a squared parasol
to shield the gladiatrix in this fateful hour
as she made her elegant, aqueous way
through the sinuous leaves on the bed of the Tiber,
then strode the asphalt to the top of the Via Paola
where Manlio waited in their usual café.

V

The Anchorite, 1965

The Orchard

Mother Anselm stood in the orchard
against the weathered lattice screen
that trained the convent's Autumn raspberries,
bright crimson plush on sun-browned leaves,
juicy now and ready for harvest.
She had been picking in silence since breakfast
and soon it would be time to return to the chapel for Sext,
her turn to set the taper to the candles,
her task to snuff them out after the half-hour of prayer,
release the aroma of quenched wax candle
into the mix of lemon polish and incense
that imbued the sisters' oak-panelled lair.

It was a decade since she had come here,
to adopt the ways of St Benedict
whose Western Monastic Rule
was laid down at Monte Cassino
and followed in Coventry too.
It had been a simple straight line
from Madeleine's plunge
from the bridge of Sant' Angelo
to the silence of this convent
in the hills at Castelgandolfo
and her seat in the choir.
Her information from home
came in letters and newspaper cuttings.
Though the Rule had been relaxed after Vatican II
and she might have requested one trip back
she found no compelling reason to go.
Her hair had greyed beneath the veil
and, along with the elder nuns,
she continued to wear
the traditional long habit,

her face inhabiting the wimple
like a medieval prioress,
but she retained about her
something of the puckishness,
the mischief of a kid goat.

The community had given her charge
of the collection of manuscripts
and the well-stocked library.
A scribe in a shrine of holiness,
she was free to pass her day in quietude,
required only to extract from her inner landscape
a response to the day's contemplative intention,
and only once was she called on to emerge
from the folds of her seclusion.

The Reunion

John Donne, 'The Good -Morrow'

In the year of the final tranche
of the II Vatican Council,
Cardinal Davouren D'Arcy of the Congo,
with all his episcopal brethren,
made his way to St Peter's in Rome.
Thanks to the faithful Josie,
now garrulously confined to a nursing home,
he knew Miss Wallace was to be encountered
at the Benedictine convent of Sant'Ambrogio
and arranged to pay her a visit there.
He did not have much longer to live
and was determined to bring their encounter
at Mount St James to a befitting end.

Once alone in the visitors' parlour,
he dispensed with the formalities of the cloth.
'Well, Venetia, who would have thought it,
that we would face each other like this
across a convent grille?
I'll call you Mother Anselm in a minute,
but you must let me use your given name
for a little while yet,
otherwise the change will be too much
for the addled brain of a man
who's been too long in the sun.'

There was a ghost of a smile
and he saw that those eyes,
rendered more potent
when framed by the monochrome wimple,
had lost none of their Glendalough allure.

'And you in a veil that looks like it always belonged.
What would Norah and Nellie make of us now,
or Josie, for that matter?
It was through her I found you, you know.
To my mind she always took
an unnatural interest in your comings and goings.'

He was answered by a chuckle.
'I see you remember.
Still, poor old soul, she's in a home now,
not able to do much for herself
the result of a stroke.'

Companionable silence.
'Ah, well, it was a long time ago.
And now, here I am,
once the civilising stooge
to a caveman of a prelate
and now strutting about in cardinal red,
hardly self-effacing anymore,
though we don't wear this get-up much
in the tropics, of course.'

His strength was not what it was
but better than it would be
and he appreciated the respite
of idle chat and lemon tea.
Malachy's library was such a long way
from where he had spent the intervening years,
it was peaceful to talk about old times.

After a while, he began to approach the nub of his visit.
'I'm so pleased to find you well and so happy.
When you were at Mount St James
I would never have imagined you in a convent,
but seeing you here now, at your ease,
it makes such obvious sense.
Dare I say, I am greatly relieved
to know I didn't make a terrible mistake
with you back then.'

He continued, loath to interrupt the flow.
'I am sorry to have to burden you with this.
I'm a dying man, Venetia.
I know I don't look it, not now,
but in a couple of months,
there'll be very little of me left.
I'll see the end of this Council in
and that'll be about it.
So the doctors say anyhow.
I'm ready to go, except for one thing,
and I'll have to ask your indulgence in this.
I want to tell you something about myself,
something I've never uttered to another soul,
apart from in confession,
and something you probably never suspected
in all the time we passed together
in the boreens around that grand old place.
May I go ahead?'

She nodded her assent.
'I'll have to put this bluntly, there's no other way.
I was in love with you.
All those years ago when we walked along the roads,
I was in love with you and I had no right to be.
I was a hypocrite,
in contravention of my vows and my collar.
If you had given
even the slightest indication
of returning my feelings,
I would have left the priesthood there and then.
I wouldn't have hesitated,
I might even have converted to the Church of Ireland
and carried on as a clergyman,
had you asked me to,
whatever my family and friends would have said.'

He paused,
'I hope to God I did nothing to offend you
in the end,'
then hesitated,
'but you were blithely unaware,
heart-breaking though it was for me at the time,
at least, I hope that was the case.
Was it?'

Her hand came through the grille and touched his.
She answered him,
for the first time in their friendship,
using his name.
'Aubrey, you gave me truth,
in Glendalough.
I found what I needed there
in your company,
a meaning for my life,
a way of understanding.
You couldn't possibly have given me more
had you carried me off.
I did dream of those things once,
but you're right,
back then I didn't dream of you.'

He sighed.
'You sent me on my way to the Congo instead.
Nobody could believe it.
How could I, with my love of the good things in life,
suddenly go off to fight ignorance and tribal enmities
in the heart of Africa,
I, who had been so little convinced
of the Church's right to proselytise?'

'And now you are a cardinal.'
Her tone was bright.

'I worked hard, I fought the memory of you.
I prayed for oblivion
and for years there was none.
Eventually though, the turmoil died down
and, as you say, they made me a cardinal,
an exemplary ecclesiastic.'

'But you are.
How else would I have found my way here?
And, by the way, I never forgot you.'

He beamed.
"Well, well, now."

'I didn't realise why at the time.
Not until I gave up the world, in fact.
One day I was standing in the orchard
and it came to me.
Much too late for either of us.
I think I had just taken my final vows.'

'So the last release from the world
brought out a clandestine truth.
Oh, Venetia, I wonder what it would have been like
if we had loved each other in the usual way,
the way we surrendered.
Do you know the Donne poem?
If ever any beauty I did see,
which I desired, and got,
'twas but a dream of thee.
I once thought that might have been us.'

'Have you been happy,
I mean, otherwise?'

'I have known the satisfaction of a job well done.
I have moderated, as best I could, the Church's regime
to take account of the way my people live,
what they believe and what they need.
My brother cardinals see me as a dangerous radical,
so there's no fear of my becoming the first Irish Pope.'

She laughed.
'You would make a very wise one.
Pope Kevin I, maybe,
in homage to his foundation at Glendalough?'

'And Josie Dalton could keep Mount St James
and the surrounding townlands alight
with stories and imprecations about Our Holiness
for years and generations to come!'

'She writes occasionally to me as well.
She might be confined to a wheelchair now,
but all the rest of her faculties appear to be intact.
She was very good to the Misses Hassett in her time,
the Lord have mercy on them.'

'But not so good to anyone who crossed her path
or her clean floor.
That poor brother-in-law of hers,
Séamas Doherty, had a dog's life of it at times.'

'He's gone as well now.'

A silence fell at last,
long and companionable.
They let it sit between them
until the bell rang for prayers.

'And now I hear that I must take my leave of you.
I won't stay to Vespers if the sisters don't mind.
I have to conserve my energies for the trip back
and the long day tomorrow.
I didn't even say goodbye the last time.
You can take this as an improvement.'

The Reward

He did not proffer his ring to be kissed,
instead he gave her hand one last squeeze
and became the cardinal again.
She bowed her head.

'Goodbye, Mother Anselm.
I'll give you my blessing,
a parting gift from an unworthy
but unburdened priest.

May God bless you and keep you in His care
until He calls you to Himself in the next world.'

The Ascent

A few months later,
Mother Anselm stood in the orchard again
and held the ends of her Benedictine veil aloft,
a black and white baldaquin this time
to secure that most precious of souls
where it belonged.

References

Brendan Kennelly, *Love of Ireland: Poems from the Irish* (Dublin: Mercier Press, 1989).

W.B. Yeats, *The Wind Among the Reeds* (London: Elkin Matthews, 1899).

John Donne, *Songs and Sonnets* (London: John Marriot, 1633).

Camille, directed by George Cukor, MGM 1936, loosely based on the novel by Alexandre Dumas, *fils*, *The Lady of the Camelias* (1848), later adapted by the author for the stage (1852).

The Crock of Gold (1912), a novel by James Stephens, deals with the world of the Irish fairies with a twinkle and a touch of *fin-de-siècle* esoterica.

Debrett's Peerage, Baronetage, Knightage and Companionage, ed. Arthur G.M. Hesilrige (London: Dean & Son, 1932, 219th ed., first published in 1769), the bible of the upper classes for over two centuries, now on-line.

Middlemarch by George Eliot was published in 1871/2 but set in 1829-32. Will Ladislaw would need to have gone to fight for queen and country in Ghana, during the first Anglo-Ashanti War, 1824-31, to be true to Eliot's setting.

Mogambo, directed by John Ford (MGM 1953), though set in Kenya has a soundtrack of African music recorded in the Congo. It stars three Hollywood legends: Clark Gable, Ava Gardner and Grace Kelly with a love triangle plot that unfolds against a backdrop of big game hunting.

Roman Holiday, directed by William Wyler (Paramount 1953) was
   Audrey Hepburn's first Hollywood film and she won the best
   actress Oscar for it. The film was made on location, mainly in
   Rome. She plays a visiting princess who enjoys the sights,
   incognita, for a brief period in the company of an American
   journalist played by Gregory Peck.

Three Coins in the Fountain, directed by Jean Negulesco (Twentieth
   Century Fox 1954) was filmed in Rome and Venice and presents
   the romantic ups and downs, all leading to marriage, of three
   American secretaries, two of whom share a flat in a Roman villa.
   The film's eponymous theme song (music by Jule Styne, lyrics
   by Sammy Cahn) was recorded by Frank Sinatra (uncredited on
   the film) and became an instant classic.

Notes

All-Ireland Hurling Championship final. This match was traditionally held on the first Sunday in September. Since the late nineteenth century, when Gaelic games were codified and organised into townland then county teams, the game of hurling, played with a wooden stick or hurley and a small leather ball, has been the second most popular of the two Gaelic field sports, the other game, Gaelic football being more widely played. In the 1940s, the All-Ireland finalists would be the two county teams to have won their provincial championships and then defeated another provincial champion in a semi-final.

André Chénier (1762-1794) was a poet and moderate monarchist executed in the chaos of the end of the Reign of Terror following the French Revolution.

Ascendancy estates. The fictional Ragnallstown is typical of estates held by Norman families in Ireland since the invasion in 1169. These Norman conquerors were Catholic and their dynasties became Gaelic over the centuries. The prefix Fitz, most famously seen in the Fitzgerald earls of Kildare, suggested a Norman ancestor. When Henry VIII repudiated Rome in 1534 many of the Gaelic lords agreed to convert to Anglicanism in order to retain their lands and privileges under a surrender and re-grant system. Those who chose not to were dispossessed. This Protestant ruling class became known as the Ascendancy. In the wake of the First World War, the Ascendancy estates, just like those in England, Wales and Scotland, had to re-invent themselves by starting new businesses or face ruin. Ragnallstown developed its stud, taking advantage of the international reputation of Irish thoroughbred horseflesh.

Boreen. A small country road or lane.

Buffo. This term indicates a clown or a clownish character on stage. It is usually used to denote a comic figure in nineteenth-century Italian opera but can be used more broadly as a term of disparagement.

Cola di Rienzo (Nicola Gabrini 1313-1354), a commoner of urban working-class stock, rose to become self-styled Tribune of Rome from May to December 1347, expelling the ruling aristocratic families and imposing himself as a dictator with a quasi-mystical mission to unify Italy. He attempted to re-take power in August 1354 but was quickly ousted in October. In 1347 he had fled the city successfully disguised as a monk. He attempted the same ploy in October 1354, this time in the garb of a gardener, but his love of luxury, evidenced in the fine rings on his fingers, betrayed him to an enraged mob. His brief rule has been seen as a forerunner of twentieth-century Italian Fascism and indeed the Nazi ambition to bring the German-speaking peoples together into a single nation.

Coventry Cathedral. Coventry had not had an Anglican cathedral between 1539 and 1918. St Mary's Priory, a Benedictine foundation with a Gothic cathedral was razed in 1539 during the English Reformation. The parish church of St Michael, built in the late fourteenth century, was elevated to cathedral status in 1918 and this is the building that was destroyed in a German bombing raid in November 1940.

Croke Park is the Gaelic Athletic Association stadium in Dublin, the venue for all major national final matches.

Cúchulainn is the hero of the Ulster cycle of Gaelic legends which may date back to the seventh century. The young man Setanta acquires a *nom-de-guerre* which identifies him as the hound (*cú*) of Culann, after killing Culann's guard dog and offering to take the animal's place in reparation. He is the nephew of the high king Conchúr (Conor) Mac Neasa and leads the defence of his province, Ulster, against attacks from Connacht, ruled by Queen Medbh (Maeve). Seánie confuses Conchúr Mac Neasa with Cormac Mac Airt, the high king mentioned in the later Fianna cycle.

Ditch. In Ireland a ditch is a large ha-ha, a ridge of earth raised at the side of a road or a field, often with shrubs and trees growing out of it.

The Emergency. In Ireland a State of Emergency was declared immediately after the outbreak of war in September 1939. Formally neutral, during what was commonly referred to as 'the Emergency', Irish people in their thousands contributed to the British war effort by enlisting in the British Armed Forces and carrying out other duties in the UK, such as Venetia's ARP work. Ireland experienced food rationing, restrictions on movement and blackouts in common with the UK.

Fidalga. This word denotes a woman of the Portuguese gentry. Maria Amalia's surnames indicate three different linguistic heritages: the names Mendes and da Silva are Portuguese, Mendoza is one of the great Spanish (Castilian) aristocratic surnames and Perelló is Catalan.

Fionn and the Fianna. These tales about a band of warriors under their leader Fionn Mac Cumhaill (McCool) were first recorded at the end of the first millennium and can be found in Irish, Scots and Manx folklore and early medieval texts. The historical high king, Cormac Mac Airt appears in some of the episodes. The Hill of Howth, on a peninsula north of Dublin city, is one of the most important locations in the tales of Fionn Mac Cumhaill and the Fianna. Shrathancrur is pronounced without the 't'.

Flâneur. This term usually refers to literary or artistic types wandering around the great cosmopolitan cities, notably Paris, in search of inspiration or simply procrastinating, most frequently during the nineteenth and early twentieth centuries.

Glendalough is a late sixth-century monastic settlement established by St Kevin in the Glendalough valley in Co. Wicklow. St Kevin lived as a hermit in a small cave away from the main cluster of monastic buildings which housed a conventional religious community. The Celtic Church fostered a range of types of monastic life, some of these being convents with both male and female houses.

Gligareen is probably from the Gaelic word *gliogaire* meaning a somewhat silly chatterbox.

Haggard. An orchard cum kitchen garden.

Ireland in 1938. The centre-right Fiánna Fáil party, with a strongly rural, working-class and Catholic base, led by the half-Spanish patriarch of Irish Catholic society, Eamon de Valera, formed a minority government in 1932. In this same year, the Dublin Eucharistic congress symbolically sealed the Catholic identity of the young Irish state. De Valera achieved a majority in the June 1938 general election while the first presidential election in that same year brought Douglas Hyde, a prominent political figure, revered scholar of Gaelic culture and the son of a Church of Ireland minister, to office. Hyde's position as titular head of state, while offering some recognition of the Protestant contribution to Irish nationalism and cultural development, in actual fact did little to stem the rapid decline in the Protestant population of Ireland, both working class and gentry. At Ragnallstown, all the staff apart from Grace Traynor are Catholic. This was not always the case. Very often these houses also had some domestic and estate staff who were Church of Ireland but they were usually in the minority.

Mass Rock. Under the Penal Laws, brought into being in the British Isles from the seventeenth century onwards to force conversion to Anglicanism, Catholic worship was largely forbidden, as was Catholic education. In response to this, in Ireland, Masses were said out in the countryside, often using a flat rock as an altar, and informal schools, known as hedge schools, were organised outdoors to deliver schooling through the medium of the Irish language.

The Liberties is an inner city area of Dublin, originally to the west of the Norman settlement and outside the jurisdiction of its corporation and guilds. It was a centre for weaving, silverwork, tanning and brewing in the eighteenth and nineteenth centuries. In those times, workers' families lived in slum conditions and this poverty continued well into the twentieth century.

The Charge of the Light Brigade, immortalised by the then poet Laureate, Alfred, Lord Tennyson, was an action during the Battle of Balaclava (Crimean War 1853-1856) on October 25th 1854 in which British light dragoons, hussars and lancers wielding sabres and lances with no body armour were sent onto entrenched Russian artillery with the inevitable loss of life to man and beast. It is likely the cavalry charge on the artillery positions was undertaken in error. Tennyson's poem was published in December of that year.

The Battle of Midway took place in June 1942. Midway Atoll is geographically part of the Hawaii archipelago but not U.S. territory. The American navy inflicted a significant defeat on the Japanese, suffering over 300 casualties. Ten times as many men were lost on the Japanese side.

Pangur Bán is a poem in Old Irish found in the margins of a ninth-century primer containing grammar and hymn texts in Latin. It was probably written by an Irish scribe at Reichenau Abbey on Lake Constance.

Ponte di Sant'Angelo. The *Pons Aelius*, completed in the reign of Hadrian, was decorated by successive sixteenth and seventeenth-century popes with statues of angels punctuating the parapet on either side across the span of the bridge. Gian Lorenzo Bernini (1598-1680) was commissioned by Pope Clement IX (Giulio Rospigliosi) in 1669 to design a series of angels associated with the Passion of Christ to replace those already on the bridge which were in disrepair. Bernini sculpted two of these himself with his son, Paolo: an angel with the crown of thorns and another with a scroll on which the superscription

INRI is written. Clement decided these were too beautiful to be exposed to the elements and kept them for himself.

Pope Paul IV (Giovanni Montini) was elected to the papacy in June 1963 and oversaw the second, third and fourth sessions of the II Vatican Council, with the final meeting taking place from September to December 1965.

St James the Great is the patron saint of Spain and the medieval Christian Reconquest of Islamic Iberia.

Thomism is the school of thought derived from the work of the Italian Dominican, Thomas Aquinas (1225-1274). Aquinas built his theology on the work of the Ancient Greek philosopher Aristotle but also consulted the writings of other Classical philosophers and Jewish and Islamic thinkers.

Acknowledgements

I would like to thank Mary Moloney and Máire Holmes, critical friends to this narrative.

Ingram Content Group UK Ltd.
Milton Keynes UK
UKHW012105050723
424591UK00004B/281